ROYAL
SHAKESPE
COMPANY

THE TAMER TAMED
JOHN FLETCHER

THIS EDITION PREPARED FOR THE
ROYAL SHAKESPEARE COMPANY

NICK HERN BOOKS
LONDON
www.nickhernbooks.co.uk

OTHER NHB/RSC TITLES

William Shakespeare
EDWARD III

Jonson, Marston and Chapman
EASTWARD HO!

John Marston
THE MALCONTENT

John Fletcher
THE ISLAND PRINCESS

Philip Massinger
THE ROMAN ACTOR

This edition of *The Tamer Tamed*
first published in Great Britain in 2003
as a paperback original by
Nick Hern Books Limited
14 Larden Road, London W3 7ST
in association with the
Royal Shakespeare Company

Cover design by Ned Hoste, 2H
Typeset by Country Setting, Kingsdown, Kent CT14 8ES
Printed by Biddles of Guildford

A CIP catalogue record for this book is available from
the British Library

ISBN 1 85459 739 6

THE ROYAL SHAKESPEARE COMPANY

The Royal Shakespeare Company is one of the world's best-known theatre ensembles.

The Company is widely regarded as one of the most important interpreters of Shakespeare and other dramatists. Today the RSC is at the leading edge of classical theatre, with an international reputation for artistic excellence, accessibility and high quality live performance.

Our mission at the Royal Shakespeare Company is to create outstanding theatre relevant to our times through the work of Shakespeare, other Renaissance dramatists, international and contemporary writers. Every year the Company plays to a million theatregoers at 2,000 performances, including over 50 weeks of UK and international touring.

We want to give as many people as possible, from all walks of life, a richer and fuller understanding and enjoyment of language and theatre. Through education and outreach programmes we continually strive to engage people with the experience of live performance.

The RSC's touchstone is the work of William Shakespeare. We are committed to presenting the widest range of Shakespeare's plays and demonstrating through performance the international and enduring appeal of his plays. We also want to inspire contemporary writers with the ambition of the Renaissance stage, presenting new plays alongside classical theatre.

The Company's roots in Stratford-upon-Avon stretch back to the nineteenth century. However, since the 1960s the RSC's work in Stratford has been complemented by a regular presence in London. But Stratford and London are only part of the story. Over 25 years of residency in the city of Newcastle upon Tyne have forged a profound link between RSC artists and audiences in the north east of England. Many of our productions also visit major regional theatres around Britain. And our annual regional tour sets up its own travelling auditorium in community centres, sport halls and schools in towns throughout the UK without access to professional theatre.

While the UK is the home of the Company, our audiences are global. The company regularly plays to enthusiastic theatregoers in other parts of Europe, across the United States, the Americas, Asia and Australasia. The RSC is proud of its relationships with partnering organisations in other countries, particularly in America.

Despite continual change, the RSC today is still at heart an ensemble Company. The continuation of this great tradition informs the work of all members of the Company. Directors, actors, dramatists and theatre practitioners all collaborate in the creation of the RSC's distinctive and unmistakable approach to theatre.

A PARTNERSHIP WITH THE RSC

The RSC is immensely grateful for the valuable support of its corporate sponsors and individual and charitable donors. Their generosity helps fund a range of initiatives such as actor training, education workshops and access to our performances for all members of society.

The RSC is renowned throughout the world as one of the finest arts brands. A corporate partnership offers unique and creative opportunities, both nationally and internationally, and benefits from our long and distinguished record of maintaining and developing relationships. Reaching over one million theatregoers a year, our Corporate Partnership programme progresses from Corporate Membership to Business Partnership to Season Sponsor to Title Sponsor, and offers the following benefits: extensive crediting and association; prestigious corporate hospitality; marketing and promotional initiatives; corporate citizenship and business networking opportunities. Our commitment to education, new writing and access provides a diverse portfolio of projects which offer new and exciting ways to develop partnerships which are non-traditional and mutually beneficial.

As an individual you may wish to support the work of the RSC through membership of the RSC Patrons. For as little as £21 per month you can join a cast drawn from our audience and the worlds of theatre, film, politics and business. Alternatively, the gift of a legacy to the RSC would enable the company to maintain and increase new artistic and educational work with children and adults through the Acting and Education Funds.

For information about corporate partnership with the RSC, please contact Victoria Okotie, Head of Corporate Partnerships, 1 Earlham Street, London WC2H 9LL Tel: **44 (0) 207 845 0509**. e-mail: **victoria.okotie@rsc.org.uk**

For information on Trust and Foundations, Gifts of Shares, RSC America Inc and Legacies, please contact Graeme Williamson, Trust and Foundation Manager, Royal Shakespeare Theatre, Waterside, Stratford-upon-Avon CV37 6BB Tel: **44 (0) 1789 403463** e-mail: **graemew@rsc.org.uk**

For information on RSC Patrons and RSC Actors' Circle please contact Julia Read, Individual Giving Manager, Royal Shakespeare Theatre, Waterside, Stratford-upon-Avon CV37 6BB. Tel: **44 (0) 1789 272270** e-mail: **julia.read@rsc.org.uk**

You can visit our web site at **www.rsc.org.uk/development**

RSC EDUCATION

The objective of the RSC Education Department is to enable as many people as possible, from all walks of life, to have easy access to the great works of Shakespeare, the Renaissance and the theatre.

To do this, we are building a team which supports the productions that the Company presents onstage for the general public, special interest groups and for education establishments of all kinds.

We are also planning to develop our contribution as a significant learning resource in the fields of Shakespeare, the Renaissance, classical and modern theatre, theatre arts and the RSC. This resource is made available in many different ways, including workshops, teachers' programmes, summer courses, a menu of activities offered to group members of the audience, pre- and post-show events as part of the Events programme, open days, tours of the theatre, community activities and youth programmes. The RSC Collections, moved into a new home, will be used to create new programmes of learning and an expanded exhibition schedule.

We are developing the educational component of our new web site to be launched this year. The RSC will make use of appropriate new technologies to disseminate its work in many different ways to its many audiences.

We can also use our knowledge of theatre techniques to help in other aspects of learning: classroom teaching techniques for subjects other than drama or English, including management and personnel issues.

Not all of these programmes are available all the time, and not all of them are yet in place. However, if you are interested in pursuing any of these options, the telephone numbers and e-mail addresses are as follows:

For information on general education activities contact the Education Administrator, Sarah Keevill, on **01789 403462**, or e-mail her on **sarah.keevill @rsc.org.uk.**

To find out about backstage tours, please contact our Tour Manager, Anne Tippett on **01789 403405**, or e-mail her on **theatre.tours@rsc.org.uk.**

STAY IN TOUCH

For up-to-date news on the RSC, our productions and education work visit the RSC's official web site: **www.rsc.org.uk**. Information on RSC performances is also available on Teletext

 Channel 4 page 430

RSC MEMBERSHIP

Become an RSC Member and receive advance information and priority booking plus other exclusive benefits. Call our membership team on **01789 403440** for details of the various packages available, including UK membership, overseas, groups and education memberships. A free mailing list for those working in education is also available.

This production of *The Tamer Tamed* was first performed by the Royal Shakespeare Company in the Swan Theatre, Stratford-upon-Avon, on 6 March 2003. The original cast was as follows:

Petruchio	**Jasper Britton**
Maria, *his second wife*	**Alexandra Gilbreath**
Livia, *her sister*	**Naomi Frederick**
Petronius, *her father*	**David Horovitch**
Rowland, *in love with Livia*	**Daniel Brocklebank**
Gremio, *suitor to Livia*	**Christopher Godwin**
Tranio, *a gentleman*	**Rory Kinnear**
Bianca, *sister to Petruchio's late wife, Katherine*	**Eve Myles**
Hortensio, *Petruchio's friend*	**Paul Chahidi**
Grumio, *Petruchio's groom*	**Nicolas Tennant**
Peter, *Petruchio's servant*	**Oliver Maltman**
The City Wife	**Patricia Gannon**
The Country Wife	**Natasha Gordon**
A Doctor	**Walter Hall**
First Watch	**James Staddon**
Second Watch	**Branwell Donaghey**
A Maid	**Amy Finegan**
An Apothecary	**Edmund Moriarty**
Another Apothecary	**Alistair Robins**
Bluebottle, *a servant*	**Christopher Duncan**

Directed by	**Gregory Doran**
Designed by	**Stephen Brimson Lewis**
Lighting designed by	**Wayne Dowdeswell**
Music by	**Paul Englishby**
Movement by	**Michael Ashcroft**
Fights by	**Terry King**
Sound designed by	**Martin Slavin**
Music Director	**John Woolf**
Assistant Director	**Tom Wright/Tom Daley**
Production Manager	**Simon Ash**
Costume Supervisor	**Stephanie Arditti**
Company voice work by	**Jeannette Nelson** and **Andrew Wade**
Company Manager	**Chantal Hauser**

Stage Manager	**Neil Hillyer/Paul Sawtell**
Deputy Stage Manager	**Gabrielle Sanders**
Assistant Stage Manager	**Zoë Donegan**

CONTENTS

Director's Preface

In preparing *The Taming of the Shrew* and *The Tamer Tamed* for joint productions with a shared cast I made one or two minor adjustments to Fletcher's text.

I decided to co-ordinate the characters' names. For some reason Fletcher has retained the names of certain of Shakespeare's characters – Petruchio, obviously, Bianca and Tranio – but changed others, although their function remains the same.

His trusty servant Grumio turns up as Jaques, with a sidekick called Pedro. In this production, however, Grumio and Peter return as Petruchio's servants.

The fumbling old suitor to the younger sister in *Tamer* is called Moroso: we have resurrected Gremio for another 'tilt at the ring'. And whereas Petruchio's best mate in *Tamer* is called Sophocles, in our production Hortensio returns to fulfil his former function.

Otherwise Fletcher's play, with its London setting, is delivered pretty much as Fletcher wrote it.

Gregory Doran
February 2003

INTRODUCTION

A favourite notion of the 'Heritage' view of English history – and one which partly derives from film and stage versions of *The Taming of the Shrew* – is that in Shakespeare's day men were men and women were (perhaps after a little initial, misguided resistance) their contented subordinates. Yet although Shakespeare's England was undoubtedly a patriarchal culture – one, that is, where men held the reins of power and in which, in order to be taken seriously as a monarch, Queen Elizabeth needed to describe herself, famously, as a woman with the 'heart and stomach of a King' – it is wrong to assume that women never argued their own case. If women always did what they were told, there would have been no need for the massive outpouring of so-called 'conduct-books', books that instructed wives in acceptable domestic behaviour. In fact, there was a healthy ongoing debate about the role and status of women in early-modern society that reached a particular point of intensity in the 1610s. And at the beginning of this decade, a play was first performed by Shakespeare's company, the King's Men, which by echoing the sex-strike plot of Aristophanes' *Lysistrata* and by offering a retort to a long-established item in the company repertoire – Shakespeare's own *Taming of the Shrew* – pitched these arguments vigorously onto the public stage.

The Tamer Tamed, by John Fletcher, is a remarkable, irreverent, and hugely entertaining response to *The Taming of the Shrew* which parodies and inverts the earlier play's gender-politics, providing an eyebrow-raising alternative to traditional readings of Shakespeare's comedy, an alternative neatly summed up in the epilogue written at the time of a 1633 double revival at court of *The Taming of the Shrew* and *The Tamer Tamed*:

> The tamer's tam'd. But so as nor the men
> Can find one just cause to complain of when
> They fitly do consider in their lives
> They should not reign in triumph o'er their wives,
> Nor can the women from this precedent
> Insult or triumph, it being aptly meant
> To teach both sexes due equality
> And, as they stand bound, to love mutually.

This uncannily modern, even proto-feminist, play engages directly with the conduct-book mentality and negotiates a position of functional equality for women which, by the last act, thwarted and reduced as they are, the men are simply glad to endorse.

As the play opens, we learn that Kate has died and that Petruchio is about to re-marry. We also learn – to our surprise – that things were not quite what they seemed at the end of *The Taming of the Shrew*. Kate never was, in fact, tamed. Fletcher draws on Lucentio's puzzled closing line ("Tis a wonder, by your leave, she will be tamed so') to delineate a continuing struggle that only stopped at Kate's death: 'The bare remembrance of his first wife,' we discover from the opening discussion amongst Petruchio's friends, 'Will make him start in's sleep/Cry out for cudgels,/And hide his breeches out of fear her ghost/Should walk and wear 'em yet.' 'Since his first marriage,' it goes on, 'He is no more the still Petruchio/Than I am Babylon.' His new wife, Maria, is – like Kate – the elder of the two daughters of a rich man, but she has (happily, it seems, for her husband) a very different reputation from her predecessor, and one of Petruchio's friends worries that this sweet, innocent young woman has made a terrible mistake in marrying the rough woman-tamer. As it turns out, he needn't have worried. Maria, uninclined to be treated like Kate, determines to succeed where she had failed: 'She was a fool,' she says, 'And took a scurvy course. Let her be nam'd/'Mongst those that wish for things but dare not do 'em./I have a new dance for him, and a mad one.' And she proceeds to tame the tamer.

By 1611, John Fletcher and his partner Francis Beaumont had seen three of their plays successfully staged by the King's Men and had in the process initiated a generic vogue for ironic romantic tragi-comedy that would remain the dominant mode on the London stage well into the following century. It was at this point that Fletcher – knowing full well, one assumes, what he was doing – took the risk of writing an irreverent 'sequel' to Shakespeare's *Shrew*. As a tactic for attracting the attention of the company's chief playwright, Fletcher's penning of *The Tamer Tamed* was risky, but it seems to have worked in spades, since within a year he was co-writing three plays with Shakespeare – *Henry VIII* (which Greg Doran directed at the Swan in 1996), the lost *Cardenio*, and *The Two Noble Kinsmen* – and twelve months further on he inherited Shakespeare's role as principal dramatist for the most successful theatre company in London. If we ever needed proof (if his plays are somehow not enough) that Shakespeare had a sense of humour, then this is surely it.

First published in 1647 along with the rest of the plays in the 'Beaumont and Fletcher' canon (which in fact comprises a mixture of plays by Beaumont and Fletcher, by Fletcher and various other collaborators, most notably Philip Massinger, and by Fletcher alone), *The Tamer Tamed* had long established itself in the repertoire by the time of the 1633 revival. It was regularly performed across the seventeenth century and was still popular in the eighteenth, but it vanished from the stage in the nineteenth century – presumably because, as with so many of Fletcher's plays, it was simply considered too coarse to perform – and has only just begun to re-emerge as directors and actors realise its potential both as a counterweight to the notoriously awkward *Shrew* and as a fine addition in its own right to the war-of-the-sexes tradition. The current RSC production, directed by Greg Doran (who directed another Fletcher play, *The Island Princess,* in last year's Swan season), is, as far as I am aware, the first production by a major company in three centuries; perhaps more importantly, it is the first recorded occasion since 1633 that a major company has chosen to perform both *The Taming of the Shrew* and *The Tamer Tamed* in tandem. Although both plays work perfectly well in isolation, together they are a revelation.

The Tamer Tamed is a witty, fast-moving comedy of the sexes which follows the methods used by Maria and her female confederates to change Petruchio's perceptions and the perceptions of the other men in the play (most notably Maria's hard-line father, Petronius) of the role of men and women within marriage. From the start, Maria sets out deliberately to invert the action of *The Taming of the Shrew.* 'You have been famous for a woman-tamer,' she tells Petruchio, 'And bear the fear'd name of a brave wife-breaker,' but she explains that 'A woman now shall take those honours off/And tame you.' 'And I,' she says, 'am she.' Her method is to confront Petruchio with his own weapon by redeploying the falconry metaphor he used in the earlier play to describe his taming plans – 'My falcon now is sharp and passing empty,/And till she stoop she must not be full-gorg'd' – and to turn it back on him both in words and actions. As she and her militant cousin Bianca are discussing their planned rebellion with Maria's sister Livia, Maria expresses her own desires in exactly Petruchio's language, even adopting his disparaging term 'haggard' but deploying it in its precise technical sense to denote the full-grown, independent bird of prey which knows its own mind and abilities:

> The free haggard
> (Which is that woman that has wing and knows it,
> Spirit and plume) will make an hundred checks
> To show her freedom, sail in ev'ry air,
> And look out ev'ry pleasure, not regarding
> Lure nor quarry till her pitch command
> What she desires. . . .

This extraordinary speech rapidly outgrows its practical frame, becoming a celebration of female sexuality, of female pleasure, as Maria rejects the lie-back-and-think-of-England mentality encouraged by the conduct-books in favour of a sex-life – and by extension a domestic life – that will provide her with what she wants and needs. Petruchio, if he wishes to consummate the relationship, will have to realise what these requirements are and adjust himself to them.

Maria proceeds to play a series of tricks on Petruchio: she first of all barricades herself into their bedroom, refusing to let him gain access until he has acknowledged her wishes; then she takes him at his word three times in order to humiliate him into submission, treating him as a plague victim when he pretends to be ill; helping him on his way (even handing him provisions) when he says he intends to abandon her and go travelling; and finally expressing her contempt over his supposed corpse when he pretends to be dead. At each stage, Fletcher makes careful and deliberate use of the space available to him in the Globe and at court, locating the women's revolt initially on the upper stage and then enabling Maria gradually to claim the main stage too, while confining Petruchio into smaller and smaller quarters – first the upper chamber and finally his coffin. The bedchamber into which the women barricade themselves serves as an externalisation of their own bodies, as they protect themselves from the men's attempts to enter both it and them (even Petronius, Maria's father, is caught up, grotesquely, in the general urge to penetrate: 'We'll up/And rifle her,' he cries even before the rebellion has begun); that chamber serves then to unman Petruchio when he finds himself trapped within it, forced to assert his phallic manhood by blasting his way out with a gun, yet left standing as the act closes on an empty stage, impotently furious, unable to believe that he cannot master this woman as he mastered Kate.

Crucially, unlike Kate, Maria is not alone as she sets out to defy Petruchio. Where Kate antagonised everyone, including her sister, Maria has the support not only of Bianca (and, to a lesser extent, of her sister Livia) but also of women from the society around her. It is female collective action that the men are most afraid of. Faced with the signs of imminent trouble, one of Petruchio's servants says he does not like 'the shuffling of these women'; 'they are,' he says, 'mad beasts when they knock their heads together.' And throughout the play, the men are clearly intimidated by the women's verbal facility: 'she doth not talk, I hope,' says Petruchio, plaintively. Their worst fears are embodied in the marvellously anarchic procession of city and country women who come to stand shoulder to shoulder with Maria, behaving as indecorously as possible in order to outrage and immobilise the men and representing the extension of her resistance to the whole society. They are led by a 'tanner's wife' who 'flayed her husband in her youth and made/Reins of his hide to ride the parish,' a figure simultaneously comic and nightmarish, and they arm themselves with potlids and ladles and discharge chamberpots like cannons to terrify the men and 'bring them to conditions.'

In overall command of the revolt is Bianca, commander-in-chief of the Regiment of Women, whose role, again and again, is to open up the motivations for resistance, verbally extending each of Maria's personal reasons for rebellion into general reasons for women to resist patriarchal power. She is the backstage activist, the feminist separatist, always egging Maria on (to the particular fury of Petronius, her most unyielding antagonist). When Maria prays to be made sterile until she has successfully tamed Petruchio, Bianca characteristically broadens the applicability of her actions, crying 'All the several wrongs/Done by imperious husbands to their wives/These thousand years and upwards strengthen thee!/Thou hast a brave cause.'

To counter Bianca, structurally speaking, there is Livia, who, though she is caught up in the excitement of the rebellion, remains focused on herself and her own desires. Despite the apparent feminism of her early assertion that 'no man shall make use of me./My beauty was born free, and free I'll give it/To him that loves, not buys me,' Livia is decidedly wary at first of the revolt planned by Maria and Bianca; her reason for joining in when she does is chiefly due to her need to find a means to secure the affections of her comically nervy and easily-disaffected lover, Roland.

Between them, Bianca and Livia represent the two alternative paths that Maria can tread in her attempt to renegotiate male/female relations – the separatist path championed by Bianca and the manipulative path embodied in Livia – and the play plots Maria's negotiation of these options, culminating in her final humiliation of Petruchio, the successful accomplishment of which allows her at last to offer him her love: 'I have done my worst and have my end . . ./I have tamed ye/And now am vowed your servant.' Her exhausted husband can do nothing now but greet this offer with gratitude.

The Tamer Tamed provides us with a point of entry into a surprisingly complex world of relations between men and women. The play's close connection with *The Taming of the Shrew* offers us, as it offered the first audiences in 1611, a society we think we already know and then undermines our expectations through a resolute, witty woman and a series of tricks that profoundly challenge our assumptions about Jacobean society. The serious point of the play is to emphasise the need for companionate marriage – the model for intimate male/female relations that protestantism had begun by this time to develop – but there is far more to the play than the earnest promotion of social policy. In its comic depictions of female rebellion, of carnivalesque anarchy and of male bonding premissed on the fear of women, *The Tamer Tamed* offers us not only a hilarious drama of inversion but also a rumbustious twist of a tale we thought we knew perfectly well. Above all, it offers us Maria, whose triumph on Petruchio's own turf and subsequent acknowledgement of his love force us to recognise the tenuousness of the social contract by which men and women negotiate their shared world.

GORDON MCMULLAN
Reader in English, King's College London

CHARACTERS

Petruchio
Maria, *Petruchio's second wife*
Livia, *Maria's sister*
Petronius, *Maria's father*
Rowland, *in love with Livia*
Gremio, *suitor to Livia*
Tranio, *a gentleman*
Bianca, *sister to Petruchio's late wife*
Hortensio, *Petruchio's friend*
Grumio, *Petruchio's groom*
Peter, *Petruchio's servant*
The City Wife
The Country Wife
A Doctor
First Watch
Second Watch
A Maid
Two Apothecaries
A Servant

THE TAMER TAMED

ACT ONE

SCENE ONE

Enter Gremio, Hortensio, and Tranio, with rosemary, as from a wedding

Gremio   God give 'em joy.

Tranio   Amen.

Hortensio   Amen say I too.
The pudding's now i'th' proof. Alas, poor wench,
Through what mine of patience must thou work
Ere thou know'st good hour more!

Tranio   'Tis too true. Certain,
Methinks her father has dealt harshly with her,
Exceeding harshly, and not like a father
To match her to this dragon Petruchio.
I pity the poor gentlewoman.

Gremio   Methinks now
He's not so terrible as people think him.

Hortensio   (*aside*) The old thief flatters, out of mere devotion,
To please the father for his second daughter.

Tranio   (*aside*) But shall he have her?

Hortensio   (*aside*)   Yes, when I have Rome.
And yet the father's for him.

Gremio   I'll assure ye,
I hold him a good man.

Hortensio   Yes, sure a wealthy,
But whether a good woman's man is doubtful.

Tranio   Would 'twere no worse.

Gremio   What though his other wife,
Katharine, she they called the shrew,
Out of her most abundant stubbornness,
Out of her daily hue and cries upon him
(For sure she was a rebel), turn'd his temper
And forc'd him blow as high as she? Dost follow
He must retain that long-since buried tempest
To this soft maid?

Hortensio   I fear it.

Tranio   So do I too,
And so far that if God had made me woman,
And his wife that must be –

Gremio   What would you do, sir?

Tranio   I would learn to eat coals with an angry cat,
And spit fire at him; I would (to prevent him)
Do all the ramping, roaring tricks a whore,
Being drunk, and tumbling ripe, would tremble at.
There is no safety else, nor moral wisdom,
To be a wife, and his.

Hortensio   So I should think too.

Tranio   The bare remembrance of his first wife
Will make him start in's sleep, cry out for cudgels,
And hide his breeches out of fear her ghost
Should walk, and wear 'em yet. Since his first marriage,
He is no more the still Petruchio
Than I am Babylon.

Hortensio   He's a good fellow,
And by my troth I love him; but to think
A fit match for this tender soul –

Tranio   His very frown, if she but say her prayers

Louder than men talk treason, makes him tinder;
She must do nothing of herself; not eat,
Drink, say 'Sir, how do ye do?' or piss,
Unless he bid her.

Hortensio   He will bury her,
Ten pound to twenty shillings, within these three weeks.

Tranio   I'll be your half.

Enter Grumio with a pot of wine

Gremio   He loves her most extremely,
And so long 'twill be honeymoon. Now, Grumio,
You are a busy man, I am sure.

Grumio   Yes certain,
This old sport must have eggs.

Tranio   That's right, sir.

Gremio   This fellow broods his master. Speed ye, Grumio.

Hortensio We shall be for you presently.

Grumio   O my old sir,
When shall we see your worship run at ring?
That hour a-standing were worth money.

Gremio   So, sir.

Grumio   Upon my little honesty, your mistress,
If I have any speculation, must think
This single thrumming of a fiddle
Without a bow but e'en poor sport.

Gremio   Y'are merry.

Grumio   Would I were wise too; so God bless your worships.
                                        Exit

Tranio   The fellow tells you true.

Hortensio   When is the day, man?
Come, come, you'll steal a marriage.

Gremio   Nay, believe me:
But when her father pleases, I am ready,
And all my friends shall know it.

Tranio   Why not now?
One charge had serv'd for both.

Gremio   There's reason in't.

Hortensio Call'd Rowland.

Gremio Will ye walk? They'll think we are lost.
Come, gentlemen.

Tranio   You have whipp'd him now.

Hortensio So will he never the wench I hope.

Tranio   I wish it.   *Exeunt*

SCENE TWO

Enter Rowland and Livia

Rowland Now, Livia, if you'll go away tonight,
If your affections be not made of words –

Livia I love you, and you know how dearly, Rowland –
My affections ever have been your servants.

Rowland Why then take this way.

Livia 'Twill be a childish and a less prosperous course.
Why should we do our hearty love such wrong
To over-run our fortunes?

Rowland   Then you flatter.

Livia Alas, you know I cannot.

Rowland   What hope's left else,
But flying, to enjoy ye?

Livia My father's bent against us; what but ruin
Can such a by-way bring us? If your fears
Would let you look with my eyes, I would show you
How our staying here would win us a far surer course.

Rowland And then old Gremio has ye.

Livia   No such matter.
For hold this certain: begging, stealing, whoring
Sooner finds me than that drawn fox Gremio.

Rowland But his money, if wealth may win you –

Livia His money, Rowland?
O Love forgive me, what a faith hast thou?
Why, can his money kiss me?

Rowland   Yes.

Livia   Behind.
Alas, what fools you men are! His mouldy money?
No, Rowland, no man shall make use of me;
My beauty was born free, and free I'll give it
To him that loves, not buys me. You yet doubt me.

Rowland I cannot say I doubt ye.

Livia   Go thy ways,
Thou art the prettiest puling piece of passion!
I'faith, I will not fail thee.

Rowland   I had rather –

Livia Prithee believe me, if I do not carry it,
For both our goods –

Rowland   But –

Livia   What 'but'?

Rowland   I would tell you.

Livia   I know all you can tell me; all's but this:
You would have me, and lie with me. Is't not so?

Rowland Yes.

Livia   Why, you shall; will that content you? Go.

Rowland I am very loath to go.

Enter Bianca and Maria

Livia   Here's my sister;
Go, prithee go; this kiss, and credit me,
Ere I am three nights older, I am for thee:
You shall hear what I do.

Rowland   I had rather feel it.

Livia   Farewell.

Rowland   Farewell.   *Exit*

Livia   Alas, poor fool, how it looks!
It would e'en hang itself, should I but cross it.
For pure love to the matter I must hatch a plot.

Bianca   Nay, never look for merry hour, Maria,
If now you make it not; let not your blushes,
Your modesty and tenderness of spirit,
Make you continual anvil to his anger.
Since his first wife, my late sister, set him going,
Nothing can bind his rage. Take your own counsel,
You shall not say that I persuaded you.
But if you suffer him –

Maria   Stay, shall I do it?

Bianca	Have you a stomach to't?
Maria	I never show'd it.
Bianca	'Twill show the rarer and the stranger in you.
	But do not say I urg'd you.

Maria   I am perfect.
Like Curtius, to redeem my country, have I
Leapt into this gulf of marriage, and I'll do it.
Farewell all poorer thoughts but spite and anger
Till I have wrought a miracle. Now cousin,
I am no more the gentle tame Maria.
Mistake me not; I have a new soul in me
Made of a north wind, nothing but tempest,
And like a tempest shall it make all ruins
Till I have run my will out.

Bianca   This is brave now,
If you continue it; but your own will lead you.

Maria Adieu all tenderness, I dare continue.
Maids that are made of fears and modest blushes,
View me, and love example.

Bianca   Here is your sister.

Maria Here is the brave old man's love.

Bianca   That loves the young man.

Maria Aye, and hold thee there, wench. What a grief of heart is't,
When Venus' revels should up-rouse Old Night,
To lie and tell the clock and rise sport-starv'd!

Livia   Dear sister,
Where have you been you talk thus?

Maria   Why, at church, wench,
Where I am tied to talk thus: I am a wife now.

Livia It seems so, and a modest.

Maria   You are an ass.
When thou art married once, thy modesty
Will never buy thee pins.

Livia   Bless me.

Maria   From what?

Bianca   From such a tame fool as our cousin Livia!

Livia   You are not mad?

Maria   Yes, wench, and so must you be,
Or none of our acquaintance. 'Tis bed time.
Pardon me, yellow Hymen, that I mean
Thine off'rings to protract, or to keep fasting
My valiant bridegroom.

Livia   Whither will this woman?

Bianca   You may perceive her end.

Livia   Or rather fear it.

Maria   Dare you be partner in't?

Livia   Leave it, Maria,
I fear I have mark'd too much, for goodness leave it;
Divest you with obedient hands to bed.

Maria   To bed? No, Livia, there are comets hang
Prodigious over that yet. Ne'er start, wench.
Before I know that heat, there's a fellow must
Be made a man, for yet he is a monster;
Here must his head be, Livia.

Livia   Never hope it.
'Tis as easy with a sieve to scoop the ocean as
To tame Petruchio.

Maria   Stay, Lucina hear me,
Never unlock the treasure of my womb, if I do

Give way unto my married husband's will,
Or be a wife in anything but hopes,
Till I have made him easy as a child,
And tame as fear.
And when I kiss him, till I have my will,
May I be barren of delights, and know
Only what pleasures are in dreams and guesses!

Livia   A strange exordium.

Bianca   All the several wrongs
Done by imperious husbands to their wives
These thousand years and upwards, strengthen thee!
Thou hast a brave cause.

Maria   And I'll do it bravely
Or may I knit my life out ever after.

Livia   In what part of the world got she this spirit?
Yet pray, Maria, look before you truly,
Besides the disobedience of a wife,
So distant from your sweetness –

Maria   Disobedience?
You talk too tamely. By the faith I have
In mine own noble will, that childish woman
That lives a prisoner to her husband's pleasure
Has lost her making, and becomes a beast,
Created for his use, not fellowship.

Livia   His first wife Katharine said as much.

Maria   She was a fool,
And took a scurvy course; let her be nam'd
'Mongst those that wish for things, but dare not do 'em.
I have a new dance for him, and a mad one.

Livia   Are you of this faith?

Bianca   Yes, truly, and will die in't.

Livia	Why then, let's all wear breeches.
Bianca	That's a good wench.
Maria	Now thou com'st near the nature of a woman.

Maria Now thou com'st near the nature of a woman.
Hang these tame-hearted eyasses, that no sooner
See the lure out, and hear their husbands' holla,
But cry like kites upon 'em! The free haggard
(Which is that woman that hath wing and knows it,
Spirit and plume) will make an hundred checks
To show her freedom, sail in ev'ry air,
And look out ev'ry pleasure, not regarding
Lure nor quarry till her pitch command
What she desires, making her foundered keeper
Be glad to fling out trains, and golden ones,
To take her down again.

Livia   You are learned, sister;
Yet I say still, take heed.

Maria   A witty saying;
I'll tell thee, Livia, had this fellow tired
As many wives as horses under him
With spurring of their patience; had he got
A patent, with an office to reclaim us
Confirm'd by Parliament; had he all the malice
And subtlety of devils, or of us women,
Or anything that's worse than both –

Livia Hey, hey, boys, this is excellent!

Maria   Or could he
Cast his wives new again, like bells, to make 'em
Sound to his will; or had the fearful name
Of the first breaker of wild women: yet
Yet would I undertake this man,
Turn him and bend him as I list, and mould him
Into a babe again, that aged women,
Wanting both teeth and spleen, may master him.

Livia	I must confess, I do with all my heart Hate an imperious husband, and in time Might be so wrought upon –
Bianca	To make him cuckold?
Maria	If he deserve it.
Livia	There I'll leave ye, ladies.
Bianca	Thou hast not so much noble anger in thee.
Maria	Go sleep, go sleep. What we intend to do Lies not for such starv'd souls as thou hast, Livia.
Livia	Good night. The bridegroom will be with you presently.
Maria	That's more than you know.
Bianca	Good night.
Maria	If you intend no good, pray do no harm.
Livia	None, but pray for you. *Exit*
Bianca	Cheer, wench.
Maria	Now, Bianca, Those wits we have, let's wind 'em to the height. My rest is up, wench, and I pull for that Will make me ever famous.

Enter Grumio

Grumio	My master forsooth –
Maria	Oh, how does thy master? Prithee commend me to him.
Grumio	How's this? My master stays forsooth –
Maria	Why, let him stay, who hinders him forsooth?
Grumio	The revels ended now, to visit you.
Maria	I am not sick.
Grumio	I mean, to see his chamber, forsooth.

Maria	Am I his groom? Where lay he last night, forsooth?
Grumio	In the low matted parlour.
Maria	There lies his way by the long gallery.
Grumio	I mean your chamber. Y'are very merry, mistress.
Maria	'Tis a good sign I am sound-hearted, Grumio. But if you know where I lie, follow me, And what thou seest, deliver to thy master.
Bianca	Do, gentle Grumio. *Exeunt Maria and Bianca*

Grumio   Ha, is the wind in that door?
By'r Lady, we shall have foul weather then.
I do not like the shuffling of these women;
They are mad beasts when they knock their heads together.
I have observ'd them all this day; their whispers,
One in another's ear, their signs, and pinches,
And breaking often into violent laughters.
Call you this weddings? Sure, this is a knavery,
A very dainty knavery. Well, my sir
Has been as good at finding out these toys
As any living; if he lose it now,
At his own peril be it. I must follow.   *Exit*

SCENE THREE

Enter Servants with lights, Petruchio, Petronius,
Gremio, Tranio, and Hortensio

Petruchio You that are married, gentlemen, have at ye
For a round wager now.

Hortensio   Of this night's stage?

Petruchio   Yes.

Hortensio I am your first man: a pair of gloves of twenty shillings.

Petruchio Done. Who takes me up next? I am for all bets.

Gremio Faith, lusty Laurence, were't but my night now,
Old as I am, I would make you clap on spurs,
But I would reach you, and bring you to your trot too.
I would, gallants.

Petruchio Well said, good will. But where's the stuff, boy, ha?
Old Father Time, your hour-glass is empty.

Tranio A good tough ride would break thee all to pieces;
Thou hast not breath enough to say thy prayers.

Petronius See how these boys despise us. Will you to bed, son?
This pride will have a fall.

Petruchio   Upon your daughter;
But I shall rise again, if there be truth
In eggs and butter'd parsnips.

Petronius Will you to bed, son, and leave talking.

Petruchio Well, my masters, if I do sink under my business,
As I find 'tis very possible, I am not the first
That has miscarried so; that's my comfort.
What may be done I can and will do.

Enter Grumio

How now, is my fair bride abed?

Grumio   No truly, sir.

Petronius Not abed yet? Body o'me! We'll up
And rifle her.

Petruchio   Let's up, let's up, come.

Grumio   That you cannot neither.

Petruchio   Why?

Grumio	Unless you'll drop through the chimney like a jackdaw, Or force a breach i'th' windows. You may untile the House, 'tis possible.
Petruchio	What dost thou mean?
Grumio	All the doors are barricado'd; Not a cat-hole but holds a mortar in't.
Petruchio	Art not thou drunk?
Hortensio	He's drunk, he's drunk. Come, come, let's up.
Grumio	Yes, yes, I am drunk; ye may go up, ye may, Gentlemen, but take heed to your heads: I say no more.
Hortensio	I'll try that. *Exit*
Petronius	How dost thou say? The door fast lock'd, fellow?
Grumio	Yes truly, sir, 'tis lock'd, and guarded too; And two desperate tongues planted behind it With their pieces cock'd. They stand upon their honours, And will not give up without strange composition.
Petruchio	How's this? How's this 'they are'? Is there another with her?
Grumio	Yes, marry is there, and an engineer.
Gremio	Who's that, for heaven's sake?
Grumio	Colonel Bianca; she commands the works. I'll venture a year's wages, draw all your force before it, And mount your ablest piece of battery, You shall not enter it these three nights yet.
Petruchio	I should laugh at that, good Grumio.

Enter Hortensio

Hortensio	Beat back again, she's fortified for ever.
Grumio	Am I drunk now, sir?

Hortensio He that dares most, go up now, and be cool'd.
          I have 'scap'd a pretty scouring.

Petruchio What, are they mad? Have we another Bedlam?
          She doth not talk, I hope?

Hortensio   Oh terribly, extremely fearful;
          The noise at London Bridge is nothing near her.

Petruchio Lock'd out a-doors, and on my wedding-night?
          Nay, and I suffer this, I may go graze.
          Come, gentlemen, I'll batter. Are these virtues?

Hortensio Do, and be beaten off with shame, as I was.
          I went up, came to th' door, knock'd, nobody answered;
          Knock'd louder, yet heard nothing; would have broke in
                                  by force,
          When suddenly a water-work flew from the window
          With such violence that, had I not duck'd
          Quickly – who knows the rest?
          In every window pewter cannons mounted:
          You'll quickly find with what they are charg'd, sir,
          Now, and ye dare go up.

               Enter Maria and Bianca above

Gremio The window opens. Beat a parley first.
          I am so much amaz'd, my very hair stands.

Petronius Why, how now, daughter? What, entrench'd?

Maria A little guarded for my safety, sir.

Petruchio For your safety, sweetheart? Why, who offends you?
          I come not to use violence.

Maria I think you cannot, sir. I am better fortified.

Petruchio I know your end: you would fain reprieve
          Your maidenhead a night or two.

Maria   Yes,

Or ten, or twenty, or say an hundred;
Or indeed until I list lie with you.

Hortensio   That's a shrewd saying. From this present hour,
I never will believe a quiet woman.
When they break out they are bonfires.

Petronius   Till you list lie with him? Why, who are you, madam?

Bianca   That trim gentleman's wife, sir.

Petruchio   Cry you mercy, do you command too?

Maria   Yes, marry does she, and in chief.

Bianca   I do command, and you shall go without
Your wife for this night.

Maria   And for the next, too, wench, and so as't follows.

Petronius   Thou wilt not, wilt 'a?

Maria   Yes indeed, dear father,
And till he seal to what I shall set down,
For anything I know, for ever.

Hortensio   By'r lady these are bug's-words.

Petruchio   You'll let me in, I hope, for all this jesting.

Maria   Hope still, sir.

Petronius   You will come down, I am sure.

Maria   I am sure I will not.

Petronius   I'll fetch you then.

Bianca   The power of the whole country cannot, sir,
Unless we please to yield, which yet I think
We shall not; charge when you please, you shall
Hear quickly from us.

Gremio   Heaven bless me from
A chicken of thy hatching! Is this wiving?

Petruchio   Prithee Maria, tell me what's the reason,
And do it freely, you deal thus strangely with me?
You were not forc'd to marry; your consent
Went equally with mine, if not before it.
I hope you do not doubt I want that mettle.
'Tis well enough to please an honest woman
That keeps her house and loves her husband.

Maria   'Tis so.

Petruchio   My means and my conditions are no shamers
Of his that owes 'em, all the world knows that,
And my friends no reliers on my fortunes.

Maria   All this I believe, and none of all these parcels
I dare except against. Nay, more, so far
I am from making these the ends I aim at,
These idle outward things, these women's fears,
That were I yet unmarried, free to choose
Through all the tribes of man, I'd take Petruchio
In's shirt, with one ten-groats to pay the priest,
Before the best man living, or the ablest
That e'er leapt out of Lancashire, and they are right ones.

Petronius   Why do you play the fool then, and stand prating
Out of the window like a broken miller?

Petruchio   If you will have me credit you, Maria,
Come down and let your love confirm it.

Maria   Stay there, sir, that bargain's yet to make.

Bianca   Play sure, wench, the pack's in thine own hand.

Hortensio   Let me die lousy if these two wenches
Be not brewing knavery to stock a kingdom.

Petruchio   Death, this is a riddle!
'I love you, and I love you not'?

Maria   It is so;

And till your own experience do untie it,
This distance I must keep.

Petruchio   If you talk more,
I am angry, very angry.

Maria   I am glad on't, and I will talk.

Petruchio   Prithee, peace.
I tell thee, woman, if thou goest forward,
I am still Petruchio.

Maria   And I am worse, a woman that can fear
Neither *Petruchio Furioso* nor his fame,
Nor anything that tends to our allegiance;
There's a short method for you, now you know me.

Petruchio If you can carry't so, 'tis very well.

Bianca   No, you shall carry it, sir.

Petruchio   Peace, gentle low-bell.

Petronius Use no more words, but come down instantly,
I charge thee by the duty of a child.

Petruchio Prithee come, Maria, I forgive all.

Maria   Stay there. That duty that you charge me by
Is now another man's; you gave't away
I'th' church, if you remember, to my husband,
So all you can exact now is no more
But only a due reverence to your person,
Which thus I pay: your blessing, and I am gone
To bed for this night.

Petronius   This is monstrous!
That blessing that Saint Dunstan gave the devil,
If I were near thee, I would give thee –
Pull thee down by th' nose.

Bianca   Saints should not rave, sir;

A little rhubarb now were excellent.

Petruchio Then by the duty you owe to me, Maria,
Open the door, and be obedient. I am quiet yet.

Maria I do confess that duty; make your best on't.

Petruchio Why, give me leave, I will.

Bianca   Sir, there's no learning
An old stiff jade to trot: you know the moral.

Maria Yet as I take it, sir, I owe no more
Than you owe back again.

Petruchio   You will not article?
Let me but up, and all I owe I'll pay.

Maria You do confess a duty or respect to me from you again
That's very near, or full the same, with mine?

Petruchio   Yes.

Maria Then by that duty, or respect, or what
You please to have it, go to bed and leave me,
And trouble me no longer with your fooling;
For know, I am not for you.

Petruchio   Well, what remedy?

Petronius A fine smart cudgel. Oh that I were near thee!

Bianca If you had teeth now, what a case were we in!

Gremio These are the most authentic rebels, next
Tyrone, I ever read of.

Maria A week hence, or a fortnight, as you bear you,
And as I find my will observ'd, I may
With intercession of some friends be brought
Maybe to kiss you, and so quarterly
To pay a little rent by composition.
You understand me?

Hortensio   Thou boy, thou.

Petruchio   I must not to bed with this stomach and no meat, lady.

Maria   Feed where you will, for I'll none with you.

Bianca   You had best back one of the dairymaids.

Petruchio   Now if thou wouldst come down, and tender me
All the delights due to a marriage bed,
Study such kisses as would melt a man,
And turn thyself into a thousand figures
To add new flames unto me, I would stand
Thus heavy, thus regardless, thus despising
Thee, and thy best allurings, all the beauty
That's laid upon your bodies – mark me well,
For without doubt your minds are miserable:
You have no masks for them – all this rare beauty,
Lay but the painter and the silkworm by,
The doctor with his diets, and the tailor,
And you appear like flayed cats, not so handsome.

Maria   And we appear (like her that sent us hither,
That only excellent and beauteous Nature)
Truly ourselves for men to wonder at,
But too divine to handle. We are gold,
In our own natures pure, but when we suffer
The husband's stamp upon us, the base alloys
Of you men are mingled with us,
And make us blush like copper.

Petruchio   Good night. Come, gentlemen; I'll fast for this night,
But by this hand – well. I shall come up yet?

Maria   No.

Petruchio   There will I watch thee like a wither'd jury;
Thou shalt neither have meat, fire, nor candle,
Nor anything that's easy. Do you rebel so soon?
Yet take mercy.

Bianca   Put up your pipes. To bed, sir; I'll assure you
          A month's siege will not shake us.

Gremio   Well said, Colonel.

Maria   To bed, to bed, Petruchio. Good night, gentlemen.
          You'll make my father sick with sitting up.
          Here you shall find us any time these ten days,
          Unless we may march off with our contentment.

Petruchio I'll hang first.

Maria   And I'll quarter if I do not.
          I'll make you know and fear a wife, Petruchio;
          There my cause lies.
          You have been famous for a woman-tamer,
          And bear the fear'd name of a brave wife-breaker:
          A woman now shall take those honours off,
          And tame you. Nay, never look so big. She shall, believe me,
          And I am she. What think ye? Good night to all.
          Ye shall find sentinels.

Bianca   If ye dare sally.   Exeunt above

Petronius The devil's in 'em, e'en the very devil,
          The downright devil!

Petruchio I'll devil 'em, by these ten bones I will!
          I'll bring it to the old proverb, 'No sport, no pie'.
          Death! Taken down i'th' top of all my speed?
          This is fine dancing! Gentlemen, stick to me.
          We will beleaguer 'em, and starve 'em out.

Petronius If the good women of the town dare succour 'em,
          We shall have wars indeed.

Hortensio I'll stand perdue upon 'em.

Gremio   My regiment shall lie before.

Grumio   I think so; 'tis grown too old to stand.

Petruchio Let's in, and each provide his tackle.
We'll fire 'em out, or make 'em beg for pardons
On their bare knees.
Am I Petruchio, fear'd, and spoken of,
And on my wedding-night am I thus jaded?   *Exeunt*

ACT TWO

SCENE ONE

Enter Rowland and Peter at several doors

Rowland Now, Peter?

Peter   Very busy, Master Rowland.

Rowland What haste, man?

Peter   I beseech you pardon me,
I am not my own man.

Rowland   Thou art not mad?

Peter No; but believe me, as hasty.

Rowland   The cause, good Peter?

Peter There be a thousand, sir. From all such women deliver me.

                                        Exit

Enter Grumio

Rowland What ails the fellow, trow? Grumio?

Grumio   Your friend, sir,
But very full of business.

Rowland   Nothing but business?
Prithee the reason: is there any dying?

Grumio I would there were, sir.

Rowland   But thy business?

Grumio I'll tell you in a word: I am sent to lay
An imposition upon souse and puddings,

Pasties and penny custards, that the women
May not relieve yon rebels. Fare ye well, sir.   *Exit*

Enter Hortensio

Rowland   What a devil ail they? Custards and pasties?
What's this to th' purpose? O, well met.

Hortensio   Now, Rowland,
I cannot stay to talk long.

Rowland   What's the matter?
Here's stirring, but to what end? Whither go you?

Hortensio To view the works.

Rowland   What works?

Hortensio   The women's trenches.

Rowland Trenches? Are such to see?

Hortensio   I do not jest, sir.

Rowland I cannot understand you.

Hortensio   Do not you hear
In what a state of quarrel the new bride
Stands with her husband?

Rowland Let him stand with her, and there's an end.

Hortensio It should be, but by'r Lady she holds him out
At pike's end. Such a regiment of rutters
Never defied men braver.

Rowland   This is news
Stranger than armies in the air. You saw not
My gentle mistress?

Hortensio   Yes, and meditating
Upon some secret business.
Will you along?

Rowland   No.

Hortensio	Farewell.	*Exit*

Rowland   Farewell, sir.

Enter Livia at one door, and Gremio at another, harkening

Here she comes,
And yonder walks the stallion harkening.
Yet I'll salute her. Save you, beauteous mistress.

Livia   (*aside*) The fox is kennell'd for me. Save you, sir.

Rowland   Why do you look so strange?

Livia   I used to look, sir,
Without examination.

Gremio   (*aside*) Twenty spur-royals for that word!

Rowland   Belike then
The object discontents you?

Livia   Yes it does.

Rowland   Is't come to this? You know me, do you not?

Livia   Yes, as I may know many by repentance.

Rowland   Why do you break your faith?

Livia   I'll tell you that too.
You are under age, and no band holds upon you.

Gremio   (*aside*) Excellent wench!

Livia   Sue out your understanding,
And get more hair to cover your bare knuckle
(For boys were made for nothing but dry kisses)
And if you can, more manners.

Gremio   (*aside*)   Better still!

Livia   And then if I want Spanish gloves, or stockings,
A ten-pound waistcoat, or a nag to hunt on,
It may be I shall grace you to accept 'em.

Rowland   Farewell, and when I credit women more,
          May I to Smithfield, and there buy a jade
          (And know him to be so) that breaks my neck.

Livia   Because I have known you, I'll be thus kind to you:
          Farewell, and be a man, and I'll provide you,
          Because I see y'are desperate, some staid chambermaid
          That may relieve your youth with wholesome doctrine.

                        Enter Petronius

Gremio   She's mine from all the world. Ha, wench?

Livia   Ha, chicken?

                  Gives him a box o'th' ear and exits

Gremio   How's this? I do not love these favours. Save you.

Rowland   The devil take thee –   *Wrings him by the nose*

Gremio   Oh!

Rowland   There's a love token for you.
                                                    Exit

Petronius Good Signor Gremio, what's the matter?

Gremio   Your daughter, sir, has blown my nose. If Cupid
          Shoot arrows of that weight, I'll swear devoutly
          He's no more a boy.

Petronius You gave her some ill language?

Gremio   Not a word.

Petronius Or might be you were fumbling?

Gremio   Would I had, sir.

Petronius O' my conscience,
          When I got these two wenches I was drunk.
          Did she slight him too?

Gremio   That's all my comfort. She made Child Rowland
A mere hobby-horse, which I held more than wonder,
I having seen her within's three days kiss him
With such an appetite as though she would eat him.

Petronius There is some trick in this. How did he take it?

Gremio   Ready to cry; he ran away.

Petronius She is as tame as innocency; it may be
This blow was but a favour.

Gremio   I'll be sworn
'Twas well laid on then.

Petronius   Go to, pray forget it.
I have bespoke a priest, and within's two hours
I'll have ye married. Will that please you?

Gremio   Yes.

Petronius I'll see it done myself, and give the lady
Such a sound exhortation for this knavery,
I'll warrant you, shall make her smell this month on't.

Gremio   Nay, good sir, be not violent.

Petronius   Neither –

Gremio   It may be,
Out of her earnest love there grew a longing
To give me a box o'th' ear or so.

Petronius   It may be.

Gremio   I reckon for the best still. This night then
I shall enjoy her?

Petronius   You shall.

Gremio   Old as I am, I'll give her one blow for't
Shall make her groan this twelve-month.

Petronius   Where's your jointure?

Gremio   I have a 'jointure' for her.

Petronius   Have your counsel
            Perus'd it yet?

Gremio   No counsel but the night and your sweet daughter
            Shall e'er peruse that jointure.

Petronius   Come then, let's comfort
            My son Petruchio. He's like the little children
            That lose their baubles, crying ripe.

Gremio   Pray tell me,
            Is this stern woman still upon the flaunt
            Of bold defiance?

Petronius   Still, but you shall see such justice
            That women shall be glad after this tempest
            To tie their husband's shoes and walk their horses.

Gremio   That were a merry world. Do you hear the rumour?
            They say the women are in insurrection,
            And mean to make a –

Petronius   Let 'em. Let 'em.
            They'll sooner draw upon walls, as we do.
            We'll ship 'em out in cuck-stools; there they'll sail,
            As brave Columbus did, till they discover
            The happy islands of obedience.
            We stay too long. Come.

Gremio   Now Saint George be with us.

                                                Exeunt

SCENE TWO

Enter Livia alone

Livia   Now if I can but get in handsomely,
Father, I shall deceive you, and this night,
For all your private plotting, I'll no wedlock.
I have shifted sail, and find my sister's safety
A sure retirement. Pray to heaven that Rowland
Do not believe too far what I said to him,
That's my fear, for yon old foxcase forc'd me.
Stay, let me see. This quarter fierce Petruchio
Keeps with his Myrmidons; I must be sudden.
Above there!

Enter Maria and Bianca above

Maria   *Qui va là?*

Livia   A friend.

Bianca   Who are you?

Livia   Look out and know.

Maria   Alas poor wench, who sent thee?
What weak fool made thy tongue his orator?
I know you come to parley.

Livia   Y'are deceiv'd.
Urg'd by the goodness of your cause I come
To do as you do.

Maria   Y'are too weak, too foolish,
To cheat us with your smoothness. Do not we know
Thou hast been kept up tame?

Livia   Believe me.

Maria   No, prithee good Livia,

Utter thy eloquence somewhere else.

Bianca   Good cousin,
Alas, we know who sent you.

Livia   O' my faith.

Bianca Stay there; did their wisdoms think
That sent you hither, we would be so foolish
To entertain our gentle sister Sinon,
And give her credit, while the Wooden Jade
Petruchio stole upon us? No, good sister,
Go home, and tell the merry Greeks that sent you,
Ilium shall burn, and I, as did Aeneas,
Will on my back, spite of the Myrmidons,
Carry this warlike lady, and through seas
Unknown and unbeliev'd seek out a land,
Where like a race of noble Amazons
We'll root ourselves and to our endless glory
Live, and despise base men.

Livia   I'll second ye.

Bianca How long have you been thus?

Livia   That's all one, cousin.
I stand for freedom now.

Maria Swear by thy sweetheart Rowland (for by your maidenhead
I fear 'twill be too late to swear) you mean
Nothing but fair and safe and honourable
To us, and to yourself.

Livia   I swear.

Bianca   Stay yet.
Swear as you hate Gremio and find him
Worse than a poor dried Jack, full of more aches
Than Autumn has; more knavery, and usury,
And foolery, and brokery, than dog's-ditch;

As you do constantly believe he's nothing
But an old empty bag with a grey beard
(And that beard such a bob-tail that it looks
Worse than a mare's tail eaten off with flies)
An everlasting cassock that has worn
As many servants out as the Northeast Passage
Has consum'd sailors: if you swear this, and truly,
'Tis like we shall believe you.

Livia   I do swear it.

Maria   Stay yet a little.
Came this wholesome motion from your own opinion
Or some suggestion of the foe?

Livia   Ne'er fear me,
For by that little faith I have in husbands,
And the great zeal I bear your cause, I come
Full of that liberty you stand for, sister.

Maria   If we believe, and you prove recreant, Livia,
Think what a maim you give the noble cause
We now stand up for.

Bianca   Mark me, Livia,
If thou be'st double, and betray'st our honours,
And we fail in our purpose, get thee where
There is no women living, nor no hope
There ever shall be.

Maria   If a mother's daughter,
That ever heard the name of stubborn husband
Find thee, and know thy sin –

Bianca   Nay, if old age,
One that has worn away the name of woman,
Come but i'th' windward of thee, for sure she'll smell thee,
Thou'lt be so rank, she'll ride thee like a nightmare,
And say her prayers backward to undo thee.

Maria	Children of five year old, like little fairies
	Will pinch thee into motley. All women,
	Will (like so many furies) shake their keys,
	And toss their flaming distaffs o'er their heads,
	Crying 'Revenge!' Take heed, or get thee gone,
	And as my learned cousin said, repent,
	This place is sought by soundness.
Livia	So I seek it,
	Or let me be a most despis'd example.
Maria	I do believe thee; be thou worthy of it.
	You come not empty?
Livia	No, here's cakes, and cold meat,
	And tripe of proof. Behold, here's wine, and beer.
	Be sudden, I shall be surpris'd else.
Maria	Meet at the low parlour door; there lies a close way.
Bianca	Be wary as you come.
Livia	I warrant ye.

Exeunt

SCENE THREE

Enter Rowland and Tranio at several doors

Tranio	Now, Rowland?
Rowland	How do you?
Tranio	How dost thou, man?
	Thou look'st ill.
Rowland	Yes, pray can you tell me, Tranio,

            Who knew the devil first?

Tranio   A woman.

Rowland So, were they not well acquainted?

Tranio   Maybe so,
            For they had certain dialogues together.

Rowland He sold her fruit, I take it?

Tranio   Yes, and cheese
            That chok'd all mankind after.

Rowl   That cold fruit after eating bred naught in her
            But windy promises.

Tranio   Now for heaven's sake,
            Why what ail'st thou, Rowland?

Rowland   I am ridden, Tranio,
            (Heaven keep my wits together) by a thing
            Our worst thoughts are too noble for: a woman.

Tranio   Your mistress has a little frown'd, it may be?

Rowland She was my mistress.

Tranio   Is she not?

Rowland   No, Tranio.
            She has done me such disgrace, so spitefully,
            That henceforth a good horse shall be my mistress,
            And if you see her, tell her, I do beseech you –

Tranio   I will, Rowland.

Rowland   She may sooner
            Shed one true tear, mean one hour constantly,
            Be old and honest, married and a maid,
            Than make me see her more, or more believe her.
            And now I have met a messenger, farewell, sir.   *Exit*

Tranio	Alas, poor Rowland, I will do it for thee.
	I'll watch this young man; desperate thoughts may seize him,
	And if my purse or counsel can, I'll ease him. *Exit*

SCENE FOUR

Enter Petruchio, Petronius, Gremio, and Hortensio

Petruchio	For look you, gentlemen, say that I grant her,
	Out of my free and liberal love, a pardon,
	Which you and all men else know she deserves not:
	Can all the world leave laughing?
Petronius	I think not.
Petruchio	No, by God they cannot;
	For pray consider, have you ever read,
	Or heard of, or can any man imagine,
	So stiff a tomboy, or so set a malice,
	And such a brazen resolution,
	As this young crab-tree? And without a cause!
	Not a foul word comes 'cross her, not a fear
	She justly can take hold on, and do you think
	I must sleep out my anger and endure it,
	Sew pillows to her ease, and lull her mischief?
	Give me a spindle first! No, no, my masters,
	Were she as fair as Nell o'Greece, and these tricks to it,
	She should ride the wild mare once a week. She should,
	Believe me, friends, she should. I would tabor her
	Till all the legions that are crept into her
	Flew out with fire i'th' tails.
Hortensio	Methinks you err now,
	For to me it seems a little suff'rance
	Were a far surer cure.

Petruchio   Yes, I can suffer,
Where I see promises of peace and amendment.

Gremio   Give her a few conditions.

Petruchio   I'll be hang'd first!

Petronius Give her a crab-tree cudgel.

Petruchio   So I will;
And hard eggs, till they brace her like a drum.
She shall not know a stool in ten months, gentlemen.

Hortensio This must not be.

Enter Peter

Peter   Arm, arm, out with your weapons,
For all the women in the kingdom's on ye!
They swarm like wasps, and nothing can destroy 'em
But stopping of their hive and smothering of 'em.

Enter Grumio

Grumio   Stand to your guard, sir! All the devils extant
Are broke upon us like a cloud of thunder.
There are more women marching hitherward,
In rescue of my mistress, than e'er turn'd tail
At Stourbridge Fair.

Peter   They are led by a tanner's wife –
I know her by her hide; a desperate woman:
She flayed her husband in her youth, and made
Reins of his hide to ride the parish. Her placket
Looks like the straits of Gibraltar, still wider
Down to the gulf; all sun-burnt Barbary
Lies in her breech. Take 'em all together,
They are a genealogy of jennets, gotten
And borne thus by the boisterous breath of husbands.
Like the old Giants that were foes to heaven,
They heave ye stool on stool, and fling potlids

Like massy rocks, dart ladles, tossing-irons
And tongs like thunderbolts, aspiring
At those imperious codsheads that would tame 'em.

Hortensio Lo you, fierce Petruchio, this comes of your impatience.

Peter There's one brought in the bears, and fought 'em
In the churchyard after evensong.

Grumio Then they are victualled with pies and puddings,
Noble ale, sausages – and smok'd ones,
If need be, such as serve for pikes – and pork,
A bottle of metheglin. What else they want, they war for.

Petruchio Come to counsel.

Hortensio Now you must grant conditions, or the kingdom
Will have no other talk but this.

Petronius   Away then,
And let's advise the best.

Hortensio   Why do you tremble?

Gremio Have I liv'd thus long to be knock'd o'th' head
With half a washing beetle? Pray be wise, sir.

Petruchio Come, something I'll do; but what it is I know not.

Exeunt

SONG

A health for all this day
To the woman that bears the sway
And wears the breeches;
Let it come, let it come.

Let this health be a seal,
For the good of the common-weal;
The woman shall wear the breeches.

Let's drink then and laugh it,
And merrily merrily quaff it
And tipple and tipple a round;
Here's to thy fool,
And to my fool,
Come, to all fools,
Though it cost us, wench, many a pound.

SCENE FIVE

Enter Petronius, Petruchio, Gremio, Hortensio, and Tranio

Petronius I had rather see her carted.

Tranio   No, no more of that, sir.

Hortensio Are ye resolv'd to give her fair conditions?
'Twill be the safest way.

Petruchio   I am distracted.
Would I had run my head into a halter
When I first woo'd her! If I offer peace,
She'll urge her own conditions, that's the devil.

Hortensio Why say she do?

Petruchio   Say I am made an ass, then;
I know her aim. May I with reputation
(Answer me this) with safety of mine honour,
After the mighty manage of my first wife,
Which was indeed a fury to this filly,
After my twelve strong labours to reclaim her,
Which would have made Don Hercules horn-mad,
Suffer this Cecily,
Ere she have warm'd my sheets, ere grappl'd with me,

This pink, this painted foist, this cockle-boat,
To hang her fights out, and defy me, friends,
A well-known man of war? If this be equal,
And I may suffer, say, and I have done!

Petronius I do not think you may.

Tranio   You'll make it worse, sir.

Hortensio Pray hear me, good Petruchio. But e'en now
You were contented to give all conditions;
'Tis a folly to clap the curb on
Ere you be sure it proves a natural wildness,
And not a forc'd. Give her conditions,
For on my life this trick is put into her –

Petronius I should believe so too.

Hortensio   And not her own.

Tranio You'll find it so.

Hortensio   Then if she flounder with you,
Clap spurs on, and in this you'll deal with temperance,
Avoid the hurry of the world –

Tranio   And lose –

Gremio No honour on my life, sir.

Petruchio   I will do it.

Music above

Petronius It seems they are very merry.

Enter Grumio

Petruchio   Why, God hold it.

Gremio Now, Grumio?

Grumio   They are i'th' flaunt, sir.

Hortensio	Yes, we hear 'em.

Grumio They have got a stick of fiddles, and they firk it
In wondrous ways. The two grand capitanos
(They brought the auxiliary regiments)
Dance with their coats tuck'd up to their bare breeches,
And bid the kingdom kiss 'em, that's the burden.
They have got metheglin and audacious ale,
And talk like tyrants.

Petronius   How know'st thou?

Grumio   I peep'd in
At a loose lansket.

        Enter above Maria, Bianca, a City Wife, a Country Wife,
                    and three women

Gremio They look out.

Petruchio   Good ev'n, ladies.

Maria Good you good ev'n, sir.

Petruchio   How have you slept tonight?

Maria Exceeding well, sir.

Petruchio   Did not you wish me with you?

Maria No, believe me, I never thought upon you.

Country Wife Is that he?

Bianca   Yes.

Country Wife   Sir?

Hortensio   She has drunk hard, mark her hood.

Country Wife You are –

Hortensio   Learnedly drunk, I'll hang else. Let her utter.

Country Wife   And I must tell you *viva voce*, friend,
     A very foolish fellow.

Tranio   There's an ale figure.

Petruchio   I thank you, Mrs Brutus.

City Wife   Forward, sister.

Country Wife   You have espoused here a hearty woman,
     A comely, and courageous –

Petruchio   Well, I have so.

Country Wife   And to the comfort of distressed damsels,
     Women worn out in wedlock, and such vessels,
     This woman has defied you.

Petruchio   It should seem so.

Country Wife   And why?

Petruchio   Yes, can you tell?

Country Wife   For thirteen causes.

Petruchio   Pray, by your patience, mistress.

City Wife   Forward, sister.

Petruchio   Do you mean to treat of all these?

City Wife   Who shall let her?

Petronius   Do you hear, velvet-hood? We come not now
     To hear your doctrine.

Country Wife   For the first, I take it,
     It doth divide itself into seven branches.

Petruchio   Hark you good, Maria,
     Have you got a catechiser here?

Tranio   Good zeal.

Hortensio Good three-pil'd predication, will you peace,
         And hear the cause we come for?

Country Wife   Yes, bob-tails,
         We know the cause you come for: here's the cause,
         But never flatter your opinions with a thought
         Of base repentance in her.

City Wife   Give me sack,
         By this, and next, strong ale.

Country Wife   Swear forward, sister.

City Wife By all that's cordial, in this place we'll bury
         Our bones, fames, tongues, our triumphs and then all
         That ever was chronicled of woman;
         But this brave wench, this excellent despiser,
         This bane of dull obedience, shall inherit
         Her liberal will, and march off with conditions
         Noble, and worth herself.

Country Wife   She shall.

City Wife We have taken arms in rescue of this lady
         Most just and noble. If ye beat us off
         Without conditions,
         Use us as we deserve; and first degrade us
         Of all our ancient chamb'ring: next, that
         The symbols of our secrecy, silk stockings,
         Hew off our heels; our petticoats-of-arms
         Tear off our bodies, and our bodkins break
         Over our coward heads.

Country Wife   And ever after
         To make the tainture most notorious,
         At all our crests, viz our plackets,
         Let laces hang, and we return again
         Into our former titles, dairymaids.

Petruchio	No more wars. Puissant ladies, show conditions, And freely I accept 'em.
Maria	Call in Livia; She's in the treaty too.

Enter Livia above

Gremio	How, Livia?
Maria	Hear you that, sir? There's the conditions for ye; pray peruse 'em.
Petronius	Yes, there she is; 't had been no right rebellion Had she held off. What think you, man?
Gremio	Nay, nothing. O' my conscience, The world's end and the goodness of a woman Will come together.
Petronius	Are you there, sweet lady?
Livia	Cry you mercy, sir, I saw you not; your blessing.
Petronius	Yes, when I bless a jade. How are the articles?
Livia	This is for you, sir; And I shall think upon't.
Gremio	You have us'd me finely.
Livia	There's no other use of thee now But to be hung up at the apothecary's For some strange monster.
Petronius	There's no talking to 'em. How are they, sir?
Petruchio	As I expected: liberty and clothes, When, and in what way she will; continual moneys, Company, and all the house at her dispose;

No tongue to say 'Why is this?' or 'Whither will it?';
New coaches and some buildings she appoints here;
Hangings, and hunting-horses; and for plate
And jewels – for her private use, I take it –
Two thousand pound in present; then for music,
And women to read French –

Petronius   This must not be.

Petruchio And at the latter end a clause put in,
That Livia shall to no man be importun'd,
This whole month yet, to marry.

Petronius   This is monstrous.

Petruchio This shall be done; I'll humour her awhile.
If nothing but repentance and undoing
Can win her love, I'll make a shift for one.

Hortensio When ye are once a-bed, all the conditions
Lie under your own seal.

Maria   Do you like em?

Petruchio   Yes,
And by that faith I gave you 'fore the priest,
I'll ratify 'em.

Country Wife   Stay, what pledges?

Maria   No, I'll take that oath;
But have a care you keep it.

Country Wife   If you do juggle
Or alter but a letter of these articles
We have set down, the self-same persecution –

Maria   Mistrust him not.

Petruchio   By all my honesty –

Maria   Enough, I yield.

Petronius   What's this inserted here?

Hortensio That the two valiant women that command here
           Shall have a supper made 'em, and a large one,
           And liberal entertainment without grudging,
           And pay for all their soldiers.

Petruchio   That shall be too;
           And if a tun of wine will serve to pay 'em,
           They shall have justice. I ordain ye all
           Paymasters, gentlemen.

Maria   We'll meet you in the parlour.

Petruchio Ne'er look sad, sir, for I will do it.

Hortensio   There's no danger in't.

Petruchio For Livia's article, you shall observe it;
           I have tied myself.

Petronius   I will.

Petruchio   Along then. Now
           Either I break or this stiff plant must bow.   *Exeunt*

ACT THREE

SCENE ONE

Enter Tranio and Rowland

Tranio   Come, you shall take my counsel.

Rowland   I shall hang first.
I'll no more love, that's certain; 'tis a bane
Next that they poison rats with.
No, I thank heaven I have my sleep again,
And now begin to write sense. I can walk ye
A long hour in my chamber like a man,
And think of something that may better me;
No more 'aye-me's, and *misereres*, Tranio,
Come near my brain. I'll tell thee, could the devil
Be brought to love, and love a woman,
'Twould firk him with a fire he never felt yet.
I tell thee there is nothing
(It may be thy case, Tranio, therefore hear me)
Under the sun (reckon the mass of follies
Crept into th' world with man) so desperate,
So mad, so senseless, poor and base, so wretched,
Roguey, and scurvy –

Tranio   Whither wilt thou, Rowland?

Rowland   As 'tis to be in love.

Tranio   And why for heaven's sake?

Rowland   And why for heaven's sake? Dost thou not conceive me?

Tranio   No, by my troth.

Rowland   When thou lovest,
        And first begin'st to worship the gilt calf,
        Forthwith thou art a slave.

Tranio   That's a new doctrine.

Rowland Next thou art no more a man.

Tranio   What, then?

Rowland   A frippery;
        Nothing but braided hair and penny riband,
        Glove, garter, ring, rose, or at best a swabber.
        Then thou wilt lose thy language.

Tranio   Why?

Rowland   O Tranio,
        Those things in love ne'er talk as we do.

Tranio   No?

Rowland No, without doubt, they sigh and shake the head,
        And sometimes whistle dolefully.

Tranio   No tongue?

Rowland Yes, Tranio, but no truth in't, nor no reason,
        And when they cant ye shall hear
        Such gibb'rish, such 'Believe me, I protest, sweet',
        And 'Deign me, lady, deign me, I beseech ye,
        Your poor unworthy lump', and then she licks him.

Tranio A pox on't, this is nothing.

Rowland   Thou hast hit it.
        Then talks she ten times worse, and wries and wriggles
        As though she had the itch.

Tranio   Wilt thou, Rowland,
        Certain ne'er love again?

Rowland	I think so, certain, And if I be not dead drunk, I shall keep it.
Tranio	What wilt thou Give me for ten pound now, when thou next lovest, And the same woman still?
Rowland	Give me the money; A hundred, and my bond for't.
Tranio	But pray hear me: I'll work all means I can to reconcile ye.
Rowland	Do, do, give me the money.
Tranio	There.
Rowland	Work, Tranio.
Tranio	You shall go sometimes where she is.
Rowland	Yes, straight. This is the first good I e'er got by woman.
Tranio	You would think it strange now, if another beauty Love you as much, or more, than she now hates you.
Rowland	'Tis a good hearing. Let 'em love. Ten pound more, I never love that woman.
Tranio	There it is; And so an hundred, if you lose.
Rowland	'Tis done; I am sure I am in excellent case to win.
Tranio	I must have leave To tell you, and tell truth too, what she is, And how she suffers for you.
Rowland	Ten pound more, I never believe you.

Tranio	No, sir, I am stinted.
Rowland	Well, take your best way then.
Tranio	Let's walk. I am glad Your sullen fever's off.
Rowland	Shalt see me, Tranio, A monstrous merry man now. Come, and as we go, tell me the general hurry Of these mad wenches and their works.
Tranio	I will.
Rowland	And do thy worst.
Tranio	Something I'll do.
Rowland	Do, Tranio. *Exeunt*

SCENE TWO

Enter Peter and Grumio

Peter	Are they gone?
Grumio	Yes, they are gone, and all the pans i'th' town Beating before 'em. What strange admonitions They gave my master, and how fearfully They threaten'd, if he broke 'em!
Peter	O' my conscience H'as found his full match now.
Grumio	That I believe too.
Peter	How did she entertain him?
Grumio	She look'd on him.

Peter	But scurvily?

Grumio   Faith, with no great affection
That I saw; and I heard some say he kiss'd her
Upon a treaty, but some say upon her cheek.

Peter   Faith, Grumio, what wouldst thou give
For such a wife now?

Grumio   Full as many prayers
As the most zealous Puritan conceives against players,
That heaven would bless me from her. Mark it, Peter,
If this house be not turn'd within this fortnight
With the foundation upward, I'll be carted.
My master –
I do not like his look, I fear h'as fasted
For all this preparation; let's steal by him.

Exeunt

SCENE THREE

Enter Petruchio and Hortensio

Hortensio   Not let you touch her all this night?

Petruchio   Not touch her.

Hortensio   Where was your courage?

Petruchio   Where was her obedience?
Never poor man was sham'd so; never rascal
That keeps a stud of whores was us'd so basely.

Hortensio Pray tell me one thing truly: do you love her?

Petruchio I would I did not.

Hortensio   It may be then,
         Her modesty requir'd a little violence?
         Some women love to struggle.

Petruchio   She had it,
         And so much that I sweat for't, so I did,
         But to no end.
         She swore my force might weary her, but win her
         I never could, nor should, till she consented;
         And I might take her body prisoner,
         But for her mind or appetite –

Hortensio Us'd you no more art?

Petruchio   Yes, I swore to her,
         And by no little ones, if presently
         Without more disputation on the matter,
         She grew not nearer to me, and dispatch'd me
         Out of the pain I was, for I was nettl'd,
         And willingly, and eagerly, and sweetly,
         I would to her chambermaid, and in her hearing
         Begin her such a hunt's-up –

Hortensio   Then she started?

Petruchio No more than I do now; marry, she answered
         If I were so dispos'd, she could not help it;
         But there was one call'd Grumio, a poor butler,
         One that might well content a single woman.

Hortensio And he should tilt her.

Petruchio   To that sense, and last
         She bade me yet these six nights look for nothing
         But a kiss or two to close my stomach.

Hortensio   Stay ye, stay ye,
         Was she thus when you woo'd her?

Petruchio   Nothing, Hortensio,

             More keenly eager. I was oft afraid
             She had been light and easy, she would show'r
             Her kisses so upon me.

Hortensio   Then I fear
             Another spoke's i'th' wheel.

Petruchio   Now thou hast found me.
             There gnaws my devil, Hortensio. O patience
             Preserve me that I make her not example
             By some unworthy way, as flaying her,
             Boiling, or making verjuice, drying her.

Hortensio I hear her.

Petruchio   Mark her then, and see the heir
             Of spite and prodigality. She has studied
             A way to beggar's both, and by this hand

             Maria at the door, and Servant and woman

             She shall be, if I live, a doxy.

Hortensio   Fie, sir.

Maria   I do not like that dressing, 'tis too poor.
             Let me have six gold laces, broad and massy,
             And betwixt ev'ry lace a rich embroid'ry.
             Line the gown through with plush, perfum'd, and purfle
             All the sleeves down with pearl.

Petruchio   What think you, Hortensio?
             In what point stands my state now?

Maria   For those hangings,
             Let 'em be carried where I gave appointment,
             They are too base for my use, and bespeak
             New pieces of the civil wars of France;
             Let 'em be large and lively, and all silk work,
             The borders gold.

Hortensio	Aye marry, sir, this cuts it.

Maria That fourteen yards of satin give my woman;
I do not like the colour, 'tis too civil;
There's too much silk i'th' lace too. Tell the Dutchman
That brought the mares, he must with all speed send me
Another suit of horses, and by all means
Ten cast of hawks for th' river, I much care not
What price they bear, so they be sound and flying,
For the next winter I am for the country,
And mean to take my pleasure. O, good morrow.

Hortensio Good morrow, lady, how is't now?

Maria   Faith, sickly,
This house stands in an ill air –

Petruchio   Yet more charges?

Maria Subject to rots and rheums. Out on't, 'tis nothing
But a til'd fog.

Petruchio   What think you of the lodge then?

Maria I like the seat, but 'tis too little. Hortensio,
Let me have thy opinion, thou hast judgement.

Petruchio 'Tis very well.

Maria   What if I pluck it down,
And built a square upon it, with two courts
Still rising from the entrance?

Petruchio   And i'th' midst
A College for young scolds!

Maria   And to the southward
Take in a garden of some twenty acres,
And cast it of the Italian fashion, hanging.

Petruchio And you could cast yourself so too! Pray, lady,
Will not this cost much money?

Maria   Some five thousand,
        Say six. I'll have it battled too.

Petruchio   And gilt? Maria,
        This is a fearful course you take; pray think on't.
        You are a woman now, a wife, and his
        That must in honesty and justice look for
        Some due obedience from you.

Maria   That bare word
        Shall cost you many a pound more, build upon't.
        Tell me of due obedience?
        Are we not one piece with you, and as worthy
        Our own intentions as you yours?

Petruchio   Pray hear me.

Maria   Take two small drops of water, equal weigh'd,
        Tell me which is the heaviest, and which ought
        First to descend in duty?

Petruchio   You mistake me;
        I urge not service from you, nor obedience
        In way of duty, but of love and credit;
        All I expect is but a noble care
        Of what I have brought you, and of what I am,
        And what our name may be.

Maria   That's in my making.

Petruchio 'Tis true, it is so.

Maria   Yes it is, Petruchio,
        For there was never man without our moulding,
        Without our stamp upon him, and our justice,
        Left anything three ages after him
        Good, and his own.

Hortensio   Good lady, understand him.

Maria   I do too much, sweet Hortensio, he's one
            Of a most spiteful self-condition:
            A bravery dwells in his blood yet, of abusing
            His first good wife; he's sooner fire than powder,
            And sooner mischief.

Petruchio   If I be so sudden,
            Do not you fear me?

Maria   No, nor yet care for you,
            And, if it may be lawful, I defy you.

Petruchio Does this become you now?

Maria   It shall become me.

Petruchio Thou disobedient, weak, vainglorious woman,
            Were I but half so wilful as thou spiteful,
            I should now drag thee to thy duty!

Maria   Drag me?

Petruchio But I am friends again. Take all your pleasure.

Maria   Now you perceive him, Hortensio.

Petruchio   I love thee
            Above thy vanity, thou faithless creature.

Maria   Would I had been so happy when I married
            But to have met an honest man like thee,
            For I am sure thou art good, I know thou art honest,
            A handsome hurtless man, a loving man,
            Though never a penny with him; and those eyes,
            That face, and that true heart. Wear this for my sake,
            And when thou think'st upon me, pity me:
            I am cast away.   *Exit*

Hortensio   Why, how now, man?

Petruchio   Pray leave me,
            And follow your advices.

Hortensio	The man's jealous!

Petruchio I shall find a time, ere it be long, to ask you
One or two foolish questions.

Hortensio   I shall answer
As well as I am able when you call me.
If she mean true, 'tis but a little killing,
And if I do not venture it, rots take me.
Farewell, sir.   *Exit*

Petruchio   Pray farewell. Is there no keeping
A wife to one man's use? No wintering
These cattle without straying? 'Tis hard dealing,
Very hard dealing, gentlemen, strange dealing.
Now in the name of madness, what star reign'd,
What dog-star, bull- or bear-star, when I married
This second wife, this whirlwind, that takes all
Within her compass? Was I not well warn'd,
And beaten to repentance in the days
Of my first doting? Had I not wife enough
To turn my tools to? Did I want vexation,
Or any special care to kill my heart?
Had I not ev'ry morning a rare breakfast
Of ill language, and at dinner,
A diet of the same dish? Was there evening
That e'er past over us without 'Thou knave'
Or 'Thou whore' for digestion? And did heaven forgive me,
And take this serpent from me? And am I
Keeping tame devils now again? My heart aches;
Something I must do speedily. I'll die,
If I can handsomely, for that's the way
To make a rascal of her. I am sick.   *Exit*

SCENE FOUR

Enter Livia, Bianca, Tranio, and Rowland

Livia	Then I must be content, sir, with my fortune.

Rowland And I with mine.

Livia   I did not think a look,
Or a poor word or two, could have displanted
Such a fix'd constancy, and for your end too.

Rowland Come, come, I know your courses. There's your gewgaws,
Your rings and bracelets, and the purse you gave me.
The money's spent in entertaining you
At plays and cherry-gardens.

Livia   There's your chain too,
But if you'll give me leave, I'll wear the hair still;
I would yet remember you.

Bianca   Give him his love back, wench;
The young man has employment for't.

Tranio   Fie, Rowland.

Rowland You cannot fie me out a hundred pound
With this poor plot. Yet let me ne'er see day more
If something do not struggle strangely in me.

Bianca Young man, let me talk with you.

Rowland   Well, young woman?

Bianca This was your mistress once.

Rowland   Yes.

Bianca   Are ye honest?
I see you are young and handsome.

Rowland   I am honest.

Bianca	Why that's well said, and there's no doubt your judgement Is good enough and strong enough to tell you Who are your foes and friends. Why did you leave her?
Rowland	She made a puppy of me.
Bianca	Be that granted. She must do so sometimes, and oftentimes; Love were too serious else.
Rowland	A witty woman.
Bianca	Had you lov'd me –
Rowland	I would I had.
Bianca	And dearly, And I had lov'd you so – you may love worse, sir, But that is not material –
Rowland (*aside*)	I shall lose.
Bianca	Some time or other for variety I should have call'd you fool, or boy, or bid you Play with the pages, but have lov'd you still, Out of all question, and extremely too. You are a man made to be loved.
Rowland (*aside*)	This woman Either abuses me or loves me dearly.
Bianca	I'll tell you one thing: if I were to choose A husband to mine own mind, I should think One of your mother's making would content me, For o' my conscience she makes good ones.
Rowland	Lady, I'll leave you to your commendations. (*aside*) I am in again. The devil take their tongues!
Bianca	You shall not go.

Rowland   I will. Yet thus far, Livia,
          Your sorrow may induce me to forgive you,
          But never love again. (*aside*) If I stay longer,
          I have lost two hundred pound.

Livia   Good sir, but thus much –

Tranio   Turn, if thou be'st a man.

Livia   But one kiss of you,
          One parting kiss, and I am gone too.

Rowland   Come,
          (*aside*) I shall kiss fifty pound away at this clap!

                              They kiss.

          We'll have one more, and then farewell.

                              They kiss.

Livia   Farewell.

Bianca   Well, go thy ways, thou bear'st a kind heart with thee.

Tranio   H'as made a stand.

Bianca   A noble, brave young fellow,
          Worthy a wench indeed.

Rowland   I will: I will not.   *Exit*

Tranio   He's gone, but shot again. Play you but your part,
          And I will keep my promise: forty angels
          In fair gold, lady. Wipe your eyes: he's yours
          If I have any wit.

Livia   I'll pay the forfeit.

Bianca   Come then, let's see your sister, how she fares now
          After her skirmish; and be sure old Gremio
          Be kept in good hand; then all's perfect, Livia.   *Exeunt*

SCENE FIVE

Enter Grumio and Peter

Peter O Grumio, Grumio, what becomes of us?
   Oh, my sweet master!

Grumio   Run for a physician,
   And a whole peck of 'pothecaries, Peter.
   He will die, diddle-diddle, die if they come not quickly;
   And bring mountebanks
   Skilful in lungs and livers. Raise the neighbours,
   And all the aquavite-bottles extant;
   And O, the parson, Peter, O, the parson,
   A little of his comfort, never so little;
   Twenty to one you find him at the Bush,
   There's the best ale.

Peter   I fly.   *Exit*

Enter Maria, Servants carrying out household stuff and trunks

Maria   Out with the trunks, ho!
   Why are you idle? Sirrah, up to th' chamber,
   And take the hangings down, and see the linen
   Pack'd up and sent away within this half hour.
   What, are the carts come yet? Some honest body
   Help down the chests of plate, and some the wardrobe,
   Alas, we are undone else!

Grumio   Pray forsooth,
   And I beseech ye tell me, is he dead yet?

Maria No, but is drawing on. Out with the armoire.

Grumio Then I'll go see him.

Maria   Thou art undone then, fellow;
   No man that has been near him come near me.

Enter Hortensio and Petronius

Hortensio Why how now, lady, what means this?

Petronius   Now, daughter,
           How does my son?

Maria   Save all you can for heaven's sake!

Enter Livia, Bianca, and Tranio

Livia   Be of good comfort, sister.

Maria   O, my casket!

Petronius How does thy husband, woman?

Maria   Get you gone
           If you mean to save your lives: the sickness!

Petronius Stand further off, I prithee.

Maria   The plague is i'th' house, sir,
           My husband has it now;
           Alas he is infected, and raves extremely.
           Give me some counsel, friends.

Bianca   Why, lock the doors up,
           And send him in a woman to attend him.

Maria   I have bespoke two women, and the city
           Hath sent a watch by this time. Meat nor money
           He shall not want, nor prayers.

Petronius   How long is't
           Since it first took him?

Maria   But within this three hours.

Enter two Watchmen

           I am frightened from my wits. – O, here's the watch;
           Pray do your office, seal the doors up, friends,
           And patience be his angel.

They lock the door

Tranio   This comes unlook'd for.

Maria   I'll to the lodge; some that are kind and love me,
I know will visit me.

Petruchio within

Petruchio   Do you hear, my masters?
Ho, you that lock the doors up!

Petronius   'Tis his voice.

Tranio   Hold, and let's hear him.

Petruchio   Will ye starve me here?
Am I a traitor, or an heretic?
Or am I grown infectious?

Petronius   Pray, sir, pray.

Petruchio I am as well as you are, goodman puppy.

Maria   Pray have patience,
You shall want nothing, sir.

Petruchio   I want a cudgel,
And thee, thou wickedness.

Petronius   He speaks well enough.

Maria   'Had ever a strong heart, sir.

Petruchio   Will ye hear me? First be pleas'd
To think I know ye all, and can distinguish
Ev'ry man's several voice. You that spoke first
I know my father-in-law; the other Tranio;
I heard Hortensio; the last, pray mark me,
Is my damn'd wife Maria. Gentlemen,
If any man misdoubt me for infected,
There is mine arm, let any man look on't.

Enter Doctor and Apothecaries

Doctor   Save ye, gentlemen.

Petronius   O welcome, doctor,
Ye come in happy time. Pray your opinion,
What think you of his pulse?

Doctor   It beats with busiest,
And shows a general inflammation,
Which is the symptom of a pestilent fever.
Take twenty ounces from him.

Petruchio   Take a fool!
Take an ounce from mine arm and, Doctor Deuce-Ace,
I'll make a close-stool of your velvet costard.
Death, gentlemen, do ye make a May-game on me?
I tell ye once again, I am as sound,
As well, as wholesome, and as sensible,
As any of ye all. Let me out quickly,
Or as I am a man, I'll beat the walls down,
And the first thing I light upon shall pay for't.
                              Exeunt Doctor and Apothecaries

Petronius Nay, we'll go with you, doctor.

Maria   'Tis the safest;
I saw the tokens, sir.

Petronius   Then there is but one way.

Petruchio Will it please you open?

Tranio   His fit grows stronger still.

Maria   Let's save ourselves, sir.
He's past all worldly cure.

Petronius   Friends, do your office.
And what he wants, if money, love, or labour,
Or any way may win it, let him have it.
Farewell, and pray, my honest friends.
                              Exeunt. Manent Watchmen

Petruchio	Why, rascals!
	Friends! Gentlemen! Thou, beastly wife! Grumio!
	None hear me? Who's at the door there?
1 Watch.	Think, I pray sir,
	Whither you are going, and prepare yourself.
2 Watch.	These idle thoughts disturb you. The good gentlewoman
	Your wife has taken care you shall want nothing.
Petruchio	The blessing of her grandam Eve light on her,
	Nothing but thin fig leaves to hide her knavery!
	Shall I come out in quiet? Answer me,
	Or shall I charge a fowling-piece, and make
	Mine own way; two of ye I cannot miss,
	If I miss three. Ye come here to assault me.
1 Watch.	There's onions roasting for your sore, sir.
Petruchio	People,
	I am as excellent well, I thank heaven for't,
	And have as good a stomach at this instant –
2 Watch.	That's an ill sign.
1 Watch.	He draws on; he's a dead man.
Petruchio	And sleep as soundly. Will ye look upon me?
1 Watch.	Do you want pen and ink? While you have sense, sir,
	Settle your state.
Petruchio	Sirs, I am well as you are
	Or any rascal living.
2 Watch.	Would you were, sir.
Petruchio	Look to yourselves, and if you love your lives,
	Open the door, and fly me, for I shoot else,
	I swear I'll shoot, and presently, chain-bullets,
	And under four I will not kill.

1 Watch.   Let's quit him.
          It may be it is a trick. He's dangerous.

2 Watch.   The devil take hindmost, I cry.   *Exeunt Watchmen, running*

Petruchio   Have among ye!
          The door shall open too, I'll have a fair shoot.

          Petruchio bursts the door open and enters with a gun

          Are ye all gone? Tricks in my old days, crackers
          Put now upon me? And by Lady Greensleeves?
          When a man has the fairest and the sweetest
          Of all their sex, and, as he think the noblest,
          What has he then? I'll speak modestly:
          He has a quartern-ague that shall shake
          All his estate to nothing; out on 'em, hedgehogs!
          He that shall touch 'em has a thousand thorns
          Runs through his fingers. If I were unmarried,
          I would do anything below repentance,
          Any base dunghill slavery, be a hangman,
          Ere I would be a husband. O, the thousand,
          Thousand, ten thousand ways they have to kill us!
          Some fall with too much stringing of the fiddles,
          And those are fools; some that they are not suffer'd,
          And those are maudlin lovers; some, like scorpions,
          They poison with their tails, and those are martyrs;
          Some die with doing good, those benefactors,
          And leave 'em land to leap away; some few,
          For those are rarest, they are said to kill
          With kindness and fair usage, but what they are
          My catalogue discovers not, only 'tis thought
          They are buried in old walls with their heels upward.
          I could rail twenty days together now.
          I'll seek 'em out, and if I have not reason,
          And very sensible, why this was done,
          I'll go a-birding yet, and some shall smart for't.   *Exit*

ACT FOUR

SCENE ONE

Enter Gremio and Petronius

Gremio	That I do love her is without all question,
	And that I would e'en now, this present Monday,
	Before all other maidens, marry her
	Is certain too; but to be made a whim-wham,
	A jib-crack, and a gentleman o'th' first house
	For all my kindness to her!
Petronius	How you take it!
	Wouldst have her come and lick thee like a calf,
	And blow thy nose, and buss thee?
Gremio	Not so neither.
Petronius	What wouldst thou have her do?
Gremio	Do as she should do:
	Put on a clean smock, and to church, and marry,
	And then to bed 'a God's name. This is fair play.
	Let her leave her bobs and her quillets,
	She is as nimble that way as an eel.
Petronius	Quoit your griefs down.
Gremio	Give fair quarter, I am old and crazy,
	And subject to much fumbling, I confess it;
	Yet something I would have that's warm, to hatch me,
	But not be troubled in my visitations
	With blows, and bitterness, and downright railings,
	As if we were to couple like two cats,
	With clawing and loud clamour.

Petronius   Thou fond man!
Hast thou forgot the ballad 'Crabbed Age' –
'Can May and January match together,
And ne'er a storm between 'em?' Say she abuse thee,
Put case she do.

Gremio   Well.

Petronius   Nay, believe she does.

Gremio   I do believe she does.

Petronius   And dev'lishly:
Art thou a whit the worse?

Gremio   That's not the matter.
I know, being old, 'tis fit I am abus'd;
I know 'tis handsome, and I know moreover
I am to love her for't.

Petronius   Now you come to me.

Gremio   Nay, more than this; I find too, and find certain,
What gold I have, pearl, bracelets, rings, or ouches,
Or what she can desire, gowns, petticoats,
Waistcoats, embroidered stockings, scarves, cauls, feathers,
Hats, five-pound garters, muffs, masks, ruffs, and ribands,
I am to give her for't.

Petronius   Tis right you are so.

Gremio   But when I have done all this, and think it duty,
Is't requisite another bore my nostrils like a bull?
Riddle me that.

Petronius   Go get you gone, and dream
She's thine within these two days, for she is so.
Think not of worldly business;
It cools the blood. And burn your night-cap;
It looks like half a winding-sheet, and urges

From a young wench nothing but cold repentance.
You may eat onions, but not too lavish.

Gremio   I am glad of that.

Petronius   They purge the blood, and quicken,
But after 'em, conceive me, sweep your mouth,
And where there wants a tooth, stick in a clove.

Gremio   Shall I hope once again? Say't.

Petronius   You shall, sir,
And you shall have your hope.

Gremio   Why, there's a match then.

Exeunt

SCENE TWO

Enter Petruchio, Grumio, and Peter

Grumio   And as I told your worship, all the hangings,
Brass, pewter, plate, e'en to the very piss-pots.

Peter   And the March-beer was going too. Oh Grumio,
What a sad sight was that!

Petruchio   Go trim the house up,
And put the things in order as they were.

Exit Peter and Grumio

What a hap had I, when my fate flung me
Upon this bear-whelp with her linsey-woolsey
Mingled mischief not to be guess'd at!
Were she a whore directly, or a scold,
I had my wish and knew which way to rein her.

Enter Maria

Here she comes.
Now if she have a colour, for the fault is
A cleanly one, upon my conscience
I shall forgive her yet, and find a certain
Something I married for: her wit. I'll mark her.

Maria   Not let his wife come near him in his sickness,
Not come to comfort him? She that all laws
Of heaven and nations have ordain'd his second,
Refus'd? Deny his wife a visitation?
His wife that (though she was a little foolish)
Lov'd him? Oh heaven forgive her for't! Nay, doted,
Nay, had run mad, had she not married him?

Petruchio Though I do know this falser than the devil,
I cannot choose but love it.

Maria   I dare not
Believe him such a base debauch'd companion,
That one refusal of a tender maid
Would make him feign this sickness out of need.

Petruchio This woman would have made a most rare Jesuit:
She can prevaricate on anything. I'll go to her.
Are you a wife for any man?

Maria   For you, sir.
If I were worse, I were better. That you are well,
At least that you appear so, I thank heaven;
Long may it hold; and that you are here, I am glad too;
But that you have abus'd me wretchedly,
And such a way that shames the name of husband,
Such a malicious mangy way, so mingled
(Never look strangely on me, I dare tell you)
With breach of honesty, care, kindness, manners –

Petruchio Holla, you kick too fast!

Maria   Am I not married to you? Tell me that.

Petruchio I would I could not tell you.

Maria   Or am I grown,
             Because I have been a little peevish to you
             Only to try your temper, such a dog-leech
             I could not be admitted to your presence?

Petruchio If I endure this, hang me.
             Thou art the subtlest woman I think living,
             I am sure the lewdest; now be still, and mark me.
             Were I but any way addicted to the devil,
             I should now think I had met his playfellow.
             Tell me, thou paltry spiteful whore – dost cry?
             I'll make you roar before I leave.

Maria   Your pleasure.

Petruchio Was it not sin enough, thou fruiterer,
             Was it not sin enough and wickedness
             In full abundance? Was it not vexation,
             Thus like a rotten rascal to abuse
             The tie of marriage with rebellion,
             Childish and base rebellion? But continuing
             Your mischief after forgiveness too,
             And against him
             That nothing above ground could have won to hate thee?
             Well, go thy ways.

Maria   Yes.

Petruchio   You shall hear me out first.
             What punishment may'st thou deserve, thou thing,
             Thou idle thing of nothing, thou pulled primrose,
             That two hours after art a weed and wither'd,
             For this last flourish on me? Am I one
             Selected out of all the husbands living
             To be so ridden by a tit of ten-pence?

Am I so blind and bed-rid? I was mad,
And had the plague, and no man must come near me;
I must be shut up, and my substance bezzl'd,
And an old woman watch me.

Maria   Well sir, well,
You may well glory in't.

Petruchio If I should beat thee now as much may be,
Dost thou not well deserve it? O' thy conscience,
Dost not thou cry, 'Come beat me'?

Maria   I defy you,
And my last loving tears, farewell. The first stroke,
The very first you give me, if you dare strike,
I do turn utterly from you. Try me
And you shall find it so, for ever,
Never to be recall'd. And so farewell.   *Exit*

Petruchio   Grief go with thee.
If there be any witchcrafts, herbs, or potions,
Saying my prayers backward, fiends or fairies,
That can again unlove me, I am made.   *Exit*

SCENE THREE

Enter Bianca and Tranio

Tranio   Faith, mistress, you must do it.

Bianca   Are the writings ready I told you of?

Tranio   Yes, they are ready, but to what use I know not.

Bianca   Y'are an ass, you must have all things constru'd.
Go to, fetch Rowland hither presently,

Your twenty pound lies bleeding else. She is married
Within these twelve hours if we cross it not;
And see the paper's of one size.

Tranio   I have ye.

Bianca   And for disposing of 'em –

Tranio   If I fail you,
Now I have found the way, use martial law
And cut my head off with a handsaw.

Bianca   Well, sir.
Petronius and Gremio I'll see sent for.
About your business, go.

Tranio   I am gone.   *Exit*

Enter Livia

Bianca   Ho, Livia.

Livia   Who's that?

Bianca   A friend of yours. Lord, how you look now,
As if you had lost a carrick.

Livia   O Bianca,
I am the most undone, unhappy woman!

Bianca   Be quiet, wench, thou shalt be done, and done,
And done, and double done, or all shall split for't.
No more of these minc'd passions; they are mangy,
And ease thee of nothing. Thou fear'st Gremio?

Livia   Even as I fear the gallows.

Bianca   Keep thee there still.
And you love Rowland? Say.

Livia   If I say not,
I am sure I lie.

Bianca	What wouldst thou give that woman, In spite of all his anger, and thy fear, And all thy father's policy, that could Clap ye within these two nights quietly Into a bed together?
Livia	How?
Bianca	Now the red blood comes. Aye marry, now the matter's chang'd!
Livia	Bianca, Methinks you should not mock me.
Bianca	Mock a pudding! I speak good honest English, and good meaning. Follow my counsel and if thou hast him not, Let me ne'er know a good night more. You must Be very sick o'th' instant.
Livia	Well, what follows?
Bianca	And in that sickness send for all your friends, Your father, and your old plague, Gremio, And Rowland shall be there too.
Livia	What of these?
Bianca	Do you not twitter yet? Of this shall follow That which shall make thy heart leap, and thy lips Venture as many kisses as the merchants Do dollars to the East Indies. You shall know all, But first walk in, and practise; pray be sick.
Livia	I do believe you; and I am sick.
Bianca	To bed then, come. I'll send away your servants, Post for your fool and father; and good fortune, As we mean honesty, now strike an up-shot!

Exeunt

SCENE FOUR

Enter Tranio and Rowland

Tranio Nay, on my conscience, I have lost my money,
But that's all one: I'll never more persuade you.

Rowland But did she send for me?

Tranio   You dare believe me.

Rowland I cannot tell; you have your ways for profit
Allow'd you, Tranio, as well as I
Have, to avoid 'em, fear.

Tranio   No, on my word, sir,
I deal directly with you.

Enter Servant

Rowland   How now, fellow,
Whither post you so fast?

Servant   O sir, my master,
Pray, did you see my master?

Rowland   Why your master?

Servant Sir, his jewel –

Rowland   With the gilded button?

Servant My pretty mistress, Livia –

Rowland   What of her?

Servant Is fall'n sick o'th' sudden.

Rowland   How, o'th' sullens?

Servant O'th' sudden, sir, I say, very sick.

Rowland It seems she hath got the toothache with raw apples.

Servant	It seems you have got the headache. Fare you well, sir. You did not see my master?
Rowland	Who told you so?
Tranio	No, no, he did not see him.
Rowland	Farewell, Bluebottle.

Exit Servant

	What should her sickness be?
Tranio	For you, it may be.
Rowland	Yes, when my brains are out, I may believe it; Never before I am sure. Yet I may see her; 'Twill be a point of honesty.
Tranio	It will so.
Rowland	It may be not, too. You would fain be fing'ring This old sin-off'ring of two hundred, Tranio. How daintily and cunningly you drive me Up like a deer to th' toil, yet I may leap it, And what's the woodman then?
Tranio	A loser by you. Speak, will you go or not? To me 'tis equal.
Rowland	Along then, twenty pound more if thou dar'st, I give her not a good word.
Tranio	Not a penny.

Exeunt

SCENE FIVE

Enter Petruchio, Grumio, and Peter

Petruchio Prithee, entreat her come, I will not trouble her
        Above a word or two.   *Exit Peter*
                   Ere I endure
        This life and with a woman (and a vow'd one
        To all the mischiefs she can lay upon me)
        I'll go to plough again, and eat leek porridge.
        No, there be other countries, Grumio, for me,
        And other people, yea, and other women,
        If I have need, and the sun, they say,
        Shines as warm there as here, and till I have lost
        Either myself or her, I care not whether
        Nor which first –

Grumio   Will your worship hear me?

Petruchio And utterly outworn the memory
        Of such a curse as this, none of my nation
        Shall ever know me more.

Grumio   Out alas, sir,
        What a strange way do you run!

Petruchio   Any way,
        So I outrun this rascal.

Grumio   Methinks now,
        If your good worship could but have the patience –

Petruchio The patience, why the patience?

Grumio   Why, I'll tell you,
        Could you but have the patience.

Petruchio   Well, the patience?

Grumio To laugh at all she does, or when she rails,

To have a drum beaten o'th' top o'th' house
To give the neighbours warning of her 'larm,
As I do when my wife rebels.

Petruchio　　　　　　　　　　　　　　Thy wife?
Thy wife's a pigeon to her, a mere slumber,
The dead of night's not stiller.
Thou know'st her way.

Grumio　　　　　　　　　　　　I should do, I am sure.
I have ridden it night and day this twenty year.

Petruchio　But mine is such a drench of balderdash,
Such a strange-carded cunningness. The rainbow,
When she hangs bent in heaven, sheds not her colours
Quicker and more than this deceitful woman
Weaves in her dyes of wickedness.

Enter Peter

　　　　　　　　　　　　　　What says she?

Peter　　Nay, not a word, sir, but she pointed to me
As though she meant to follow. Pray sir, bear it
E'en as you may; I need not teach your worship,
The best men have their crosses, we are all mortal.

Petruchio　What ails the fellow?

Peter　　　　　　　　　　　And no doubt she may, sir –

Petruchio　What may she, or what does she, or what is she?
Speak and be hang'd.

Peter　　　　　　　　　　She's mad, sir.

Petruchio　Heaven continue it!

Peter　　　　　　　　　Amen, if it be His pleasure.

Petruchio　How mad is she?

Peter　　As mad as heart can wish, sir. She has dress'd herself

(Saving your worship's reverence) just i'th' cut
Of one of those that multiply i'th' suburbs
For single money, and as dirtily;
If any speak to her, first she whistles,
And then begins her compass with her fingers,
And points to what she would have.

Petruchio　　　　　　　　　　　　　　　　What new way's this?

Peter　　　There came in Master Hortensio.

Petruchio　　　　　　　　　　　　And what
Did Master Hortensio when he came in?
Get my trunks ready, sirrah, I'll be gone straight.

Peter　　　He's here to tell you.

Enter Hortensio

She's horn-mad, Grumio.

Hortensio　　　　　　　　　　Call ye this a woman?

Petruchio　Yes sir, she is a woman.

Hortensio　　　　　　　　　Sir, I doubt it.

Petruchio　I had thought you had made experience.

Hortensio　　　　　　　　　　　　　Yes, I did so,
And almost with my life.

Petruchio　　　　　　　　　You rid too fast, sir.

Hortensio　Pray be not mistaken: by this hand
Your wife's as chaste and honest as a virgin,
For anything I know. 'Tis true she gave me
A ring.

Petruchio　　　　For rutting.

Hortensio　　　　　　　　You are much deceiv'd still.
Believe me, I never kiss'd her since, and now

Coming in visitation, like a friend,
I think she is mad, sir. Suddenly she started,
And snatch'd the ring away, and drew her knife out,
To what intent I know not.

Petruchio   Is this certain?

Hortensio As I am here, sir.

Petruchio   I believe you honest.

Enter Maria

And pray continue so.

Hortensio   She comes.

Petruchio   Now, damsel,
What will your beauty do if I forsake you?
Do you deal by signs and tokens? As I guess then,
You'll walk abroad this Summer, and catch captains,
Or hire a piece of holy ground i'th' suburbs,
And keep a nest of nuns.

Hortensio   O do not stir her!
You see in what a case she is!

Petruchio   She is dogged
And in a beastly case, I am sure I'll make her,
If she have any tongue, yet tattle. Hortensio,
Prithee observe this woman seriously,
And eye her well, and when thou hast done, but tell me
(For thou hast understanding) in what case
My sense was when I chose this thing.

Hortensio   I'll tell you
I have seen a sweeter –

Petruchio   An hundred times cry 'Oysters'.
There's a poor beggar-wench about Blackfriars
May be an empress to her.

Hortensio   Nay, now you are too bitter.

Petruchio Ne'er a whit, sir.
I'll tell thee, woman, for now I have day to see thee,
And all my wits about me, and I speak
Not out of passion neither (leave your mumping,
I know you're well enough). Now would I give
A million but to vex her. When I chose thee
To make a bedfellow, I took a leprosy,
Nay worse, the plague, nay worse yet, a possession.
For who that had but reason to distinguish
The light from darkness, wine from water, hunger
From full satiety, and fox from fern bush,
That would have married thee?

Hortensio   She is not so ill.

Petruchio She's worse than I dare to think of: she's so lewd,
She hath neither wifehood nor womanhood
Can force me think she had a mother. No,
I do believe her steadfastly, and know her
To be a woman-wolf by transmigration:
Her first form was a ferret's underground;
She kills the memories of men. Not yet?

Hortensio Do you think she's sensible of this?

Petruchio   I care not,
Be what she will. The pleasure I take in her,
Thus I blow off; the care I took to love her,
Like this point I untie, and thus I loose it;
The husband I am to her, thus I sever.
My vanity, farewell! Yet, for you have been
So near me as to bear the name of wife,
My unquench'd charity shall tell you thus much
(Though you deserve it well) you shall not beg:
What I ordain'd your jointure honestly
You shall have settled on you, and half my house;

             Your apparel,
             And what belongs to build up such a folly,
             Keep, I beseech you; it infects our uses,
             And now I am for travel.

Maria   Now I love you,
             And now I see you are a man, I'll talk to you,
             And I forget your bitterness.

Hortensio   How now, man?

Petruchio O Pliny, if thou wilt be ever famous,
             Make but this woman all thy wonders!

Maria   Sure, sir,
             You have hit upon a happy course, a blessed,
             And one will make you virtuous –

Petruchio   She'll ship me.

Maria   A way of understanding I long wish'd for,
             And now 'tis come, take heed you fly not back, sir.
             Methinks you look a new man to me now,
             A man of excellence, and now I see
             Some great design set in you. You may think now
             'Twere my part
             Weakly to weep your loss, and to resist you,
             Nay, hang about your neck and like a dotard
             Urge my strong tie upon you; but I love you,
             And all the world shall know it, beyond woman,
             And more prefer the honour of your country,
             Which chiefly you are born for,
             Than any wanton kisses.
             Go, worthy man, and bring home understanding.

Hortensio This were an excellent woman to breed schoolmen.

Maria   For if the merchant through unknown seas plough
             To get his wealth, then, dear sir, what must you

To gather wisdom? Go, and go alone,
Only your noble mind for your companion;
Go far, too far you cannot: still the farther,
The more experience finds you.

Petruchio   Dost hear her?

Hortensio   Yes.
I wonder that she writes not.

Maria   Then when time
And fullness of occasion have new made you,
And squar'd you from a sot into a signor,
Come home an aged man, as did Ulysses,
And I your glad Penelope.

Petruchio   What should I do?

Hortensio   Why, by my troth, I would travel.
Did not you mean so?

Petruchio   Alas no, nothing less, man:
I did it but to try her. She's the devil,
And now I find it, for she drives me; I must go.
Are my trunks down, there, and my horses ready?

Maria   Sir, for your house, and if you please to trust me
With that you leave behind –

Petruchio   Bring down the money.

Maria   As I am able, and to my poor fortunes,
I'll govern as a widow. I shall long
To hear of your well-doing and your profit,
And when I hear not from you once a quarter,
I'll wish you in the Indies or in China;
Those are the climes must make you.

Petruchio She'll wish me out o'th' world anon!
How fares the wind?

Maria	For France 'Tis very fair; get you aboard tonight, sir, And lose no time; you know the tide stays no man. I have cold meats ready for you.
Petruchio	Fare thee well. Thou hast fool'd me out o'th' kingdom with a vengeance, And thou canst fool me in again.
Maria	Not I, sir, I love you better. Take your time and pleasure, I'll see you hors'd.
Petruchio	I think thou wouldst see me hang'd too, Were I but half as willing.
Maria	Anything That you think well of, I dare look upon.
Petruchio	You'll bear me to the land's end, Hortensio, And other of my friends, I hope?
Hortensio	Ne'er doubt, sir.
Maria	I am sure you'll kiss me ere I go; I have business, And stay long here I must not.
Petruchio	Get thee going, For if thou tarriest but another dialogue I'll kick thee to thy chamber.
Maria	Fare you well, sir, And bear yourself manly and worthily, And for those flying fames here of your follies, Your gambols, and ill-breeding of your youth, I'll deal So like a wife that loves your reputation, That those shall die. If you want lemon-waters, Or anything to take the edge o'th' sea off, Pray speak, and be provided.

Petruchio   Now the devil
          That was your first good master, shower his blessing
          Upon ye all; into whose custody –

Hortensio   You had better go.

Petruchio I will go then. Let's seek out
          All my friends to see me fair aboard;
          Then, women, if there be a storm at sea
          Worse than your tongues can make, and waves more broken
          Than your dissembling faiths are, let me feel
          Nothing but tempests till they crack my keel.   *Exeunt*

Enter Gremio, Petronius, and Bianca with four papers

Petronius   If this fair repentance of my daughter
             Spring from your good persuasion, as it seems so,
             I must confess I have mistook you,
             And I repent.

Bianca   When I told her
             How good and gentle yet with free contrition
             Again you might be purchas'd, loving woman,
             She heard me, yet all my counsel
             And comfort in this case could not so heal her
             But that grief got his share too, and she sicken'd.

Petronius   I am sorry she's so ill, yet glad her sickness
             Has got so good a ground.
             [*to Gremio*] Go get you in, and see your mistress.

Bianca   She is sick, sir,
             But you may kiss her whole.

Gremio   How?

Bianca   Comfort her.
             May be she needs confession.

Gremio   By Saint Mary,
             She shall have absolution then and penance.   *Exit*

Bianca   Here come the others too.

Enter Rowland and Tranio

Petronius   Good ev'n to you, Rowland, you are welcome.

Rowland   Thank you.

Petronius   I have a certain daughter;
            No doubt you know her well.

Rowland   Nor never shall, sir.
            She is a woman, and the ways into her
            Are like the finding of a certain path
            After a deep fall'n snow.

Petronius   Well, that's by th' by still.
            This daughter that I tell you of is fall'n
            A little crop-sick, with the dangerous surfeit
            She took of your affection.

Rowland   Mine, sir?

Petronius   Yes, sir.
            Or rather, as it seems, repenting,
            And there she lies within, debating on't.

Rowland   Well, sir.

Petronius   I think 'twere well you would see her.

Rowland   If you please, sir;
            I am not squeamish of my visitation.

Petronius   But this I'll tell you: she is alter'd much,
            You'll find her now another Livia.

Rowland   I have enough o'th' old one.

Petronius   No more fool,
            To look gay babies in your eyes, young Rowland,
            And hang about your pretty neck.

Rowland   I am glad on't,
            And thank my Fates I have 'scap'd such execution.

Petronius   And buss you till you blush again.

Rowland   Well, what follows?

Petronius She's mine now, as I please to settle her,
At my command, and where I please to plant her;
Only she would take a kind of farewell of you,
And give you back a wand'ring vow or two
You left in pawn; and two or three slight oaths
She lent you too, she looks for.

Rowland   She shall have 'em
With all my heart, sir, and if you like it better,
A free release in writing.

Petronius   That's the matter,
And you from her; you shall have another, Rowland,
And then turn tail to tail, and peace be with you.

Rowland So be it. Your twenty pound sweats, Tranio.

Tranio 'Twill not undo me, Rowland, do your worst.

Rowland Come, shall we see her, sir?

Bianca   Whate'er she says
You must bear manly, Rowland, for her sickness
Has made her somewhat teatish.

Rowland   Let her talk
Till her tongue ache, I care not; by this hand,
Thou hast a handsome face, wench, and a body
Daintily mounted. Now do I feel an hundred
Running directly from me, as I piss'd it.

          Enter Livia discovered abed, and Gremio by her

Bianca Pray draw 'em softly; the least hurry, sir,
Puts her to much impatience.

Petronius   How is't, daughter?

Livia O very sick, very sick, yet somewhat
Better, I hope; a little lightsomer
Because this good man has forgiven me;
Pray set me higher. Oh, my head!

Bianca	*(aside)*	Well done, wench!

Livia   Father, and all good people that shall hear me,
I have abus'd this man perniciously;
Was never old man humbled so. I have scorn'd him,
And call'd him nasty names; I have spit at him,
Flung candles' ends in's beard, and contemn'd him,
For methought then he was a beastly fellow
(Oh God, my side!) a very beastly fellow;
At a christ'ning once I gave him purging-comfits
That he spoil'd his breeches; and one night
I strew'd the stairs with peas as he pass'd down,
And the good gentleman (woe worth me for't)
Told two and twenty stairs, miss'd not a step,
Fell to the bottom, broke his casting bottle,
Lost a fair toadstone of some eighteen shillings,
Jumbled his joints together, had two stools,
And was translated. All this villainy
Did I, Livia; I alone, untaught.

Gremio   And I unask'd forgive it.

Livia   Where's Bianca?

Bianca   Here, cousin.

Livia   Give me drink.

Bianca   There.

Livia   Who's that?

Gremio   Rowland.

Livia   O my dissembler, you and I must part.
Come nearer, sir.

Rowland   I am sorry for your sickness.

Livia   Be sorry for yourself, sir; you have wrong'd me,
But I forgive you. Are the papers ready?

Bianca	I have 'em here. Wilt please you view 'em?
Petronius	Yes.

Livia Show 'em the young man too, I know he's willing
To shift his sails too. 'Tis for his more advancement;
Alas, we might have beggar'd one another;
We are young both, and a world of children
Might have been left behind to curse our follies.
We had been undone, Bianca, had we married,
Undone for ever. I confess I lov'd him,
I care not who shall know it, most entirely;
And once, upon my conscience, he lov'd me;
But farewell that. We must be wiser, cousin.
Love must not leave us to the world. Have you done?

Rowland Yes, and am ready to subscribe.

Livia   Pray stay then.
Give me the papers, and let me peruse 'em,
And so much time as may afford a tear
At our last parting.

Bianca   Pray retire, and leave her;
I'll call ye presently.

Petronius   Come, gentlemen,
The show'r must fall.

Rowland   Would I had never seen her.
         Exeunt all but Bianca and Livia

Bianca Thou hast done bravely, wench.

Livia   Pray heaven it prove so.

Bianca There are the other papers. When they come,
Begin you first, and let the rest subscribe
Hard by your side; give 'em as little light
As drapers do their wares.

Livia   Didst mark Gremio,

In what an agony he was, and how he cried most
When I abus'd him most?

Bianca   That was but reason.

Livia   Oh, what a stinking cur is this!
Though I was but to counterfeit, he made me
Directly sick indeed. Thames Street to him
Is a mere pomander.

Bianca   Let him be hang'd.

Livia   Amen.

Bianca   And lie you still.
And once more to your business.

Livia   Call 'em in.
Now if there be a power that pities lovers,
Help now, and hear my prayers.

Enter Petronius, Rowland, Tranio, and Gremio

Petronius   Is she ready?

Bianca   She has done her lamentations; pray go to her.

Livia   Rowland, come near me, and before you seal,
Give me your hand. Take it again; now kiss me.
This is the last acquaintance we must have.
I wish you ever happy. There's the paper.

Rowland   Pray stay a little.

Petronius   Let me never live more
But I do begin to pity this young fellow;
How heartily he weeps!

Bianca   There's pen and ink, sir.

Livia   E'en here, I pray you. 'Tis a little emblem
How near you have been to me.

Rowland   There.

Bianca   Your hands too,
          As witnesses.

Petronius   By any means.
          To th' book, son.

Gremio   With all my heart.

Bianca   You must deliver it.

Rowland There, Livia, and a better love light on thee.
          I can no more.

Bianca   To this you must be witness too.

Petronius We will.

Bianca   Do you deliver it now.

Livia   Pray set me up;
          There, Rowland, all thy old love back; and may
          A new to come exceed mine, and be happy.
          I must no more.

Rowland   Farewell.

Livia   A long farewell.
                              Exeunt Rowland and Tranio

Bianca Leave her by any mean till this wild passion
          Be off her head; draw all the curtains close.
          A day hence you may see her; 'twill be better,
          She is now for little company.

Petronius   Pray tend her.
          I must to horse straight. You must needs along too,
          To see my son aboard; were but his wife
          As fit for pity as this wench, I were happy.

Bianca Time must do that too. Fare ye well. Tomorrow
          You shall receive a wife to quit your sorrow.
                                          Exeunt

SCENE TWO

Enter Rowland, and Tranio stealing behind him

Rowland What a dull ass was I to let her go thus!
Upon my life she loves me still. Well, paper,
Thou only monument of what I have had,
Thou all the love now left me, and now lost,
O bitter words, I'll read ye once again,
And then for ever study to forget ye.
How's this? Let me look better on't. A contract?
I swear, a marriage contract, seal'd and ratified,
Her father's hand set to it, and Gremio's!
I do not dream, sure. Let me read again.
The same still! 'Tis a contract.

Tranio   'Tis so, Rowland,
And by the virtue of the same, you pay me
An hundred pound tomorrow.

Rowland   Art sure, Tranio,
We are both alive now?

Tranio   Wonder not, ye have lost.

Rowland If this be true, I grant it.

Tranio   'Tis most certain;
There's a ring for you too, you know it?

Rowland   Yes.

Tranio   When shall I have the money?

Rowland   Stay ye, stay ye,
When shall I marry her?

Tranio   Tonight.

Rowland   Take heed now

You do not trifle me; if you do,
You'll find more payment than your money comes to.
Come, swear. I know I am a man, and find
I may deceive myself. Swear faithfully,
Swear me directly: am I Rowland?

Tranio Yes.

Rowland Am I awake?

Tranio Ye are.

Rowland Am I in health?

Tranio As far as I conceive.

Rowland Was I with Livia?

Tranio You were, and had this contract.

Rowland And shall I enjoy her?

Tranio Yes, if ye dare.

Rowland Swear to all these.

Tranio I will,
For by my honesty and faith and conscience,
All this is certain.

Rowand Let's remove our places.
Swear it again.

Tranio By heaven 'tis true.

Rowland I have lost then, and heaven knows I am glad on't.
Let's go, and tell me all, and tell me how,
For yet I am a pagan in it.

Tranio I have a priest too,
And all shall come as even as two testers.

Exeunt

SCENE THREE

Enter Grumio, Peter, and Porters, with chest and hampers

Grumio   Bring 'em away, sirs.

Peter   Must the great trunks go too?

Grumio   Yes, and the hampers. Nay, be speedy, masters,
He'll be at sea before us else.

Peter   O Grumio,
What a most blessed turn hast thou –

Grumio   I hope so.

Peter   To have the sea between thee and this woman.
Nothing can drown her tongue but a storm.
Now could I wish her in that trunk.

Grumio   God shield, man,
I had rather have a bear in't.

Peter   Yes, I'll tell ye,
For in the passage if a tempest take ye,
And the master cry
'Lighten the ship of all hands, or we perish!'
Then this, for one, should overboard presently.

Grumio   So we were certain to be rid of her,
I would wish her with us. But believe me, Peter,
She would spoil the fishing on this coast for ever,
For none would keep her company but dogfish
Or porpoises. She would make god Neptune,
And his fire-fork, as weary of the Channel
As ever schoolboy was of the school.

Peter   Oh, her tongue, her tongue!

Grumio   Rather, her many tongues.

Peter	Or rather, strange tongues.
Grumio	Her lying tongue.
Peter	Her lisping tongue.
Grumio	Her long tongue.
Peter	Her lawless tongue.
Grumio	Her loud tongue.
Peter	Lic'rice tongue –
Grumio	And many stranger tongues than ever Babel had.

Enter Hortensio

Hortensio Home with your stuff again; the journey's ended.

Grumio What does your worship mean?

Hortensio Your master – O Petruchio! – O poor fellows!

Peter O, Grumio, Grumio!

Hortensio   O, your master's dead,
His body coming back; his wife, his devil,
The grief of her –

Grumio   Has kill'd him?

Hortensio   Kill'd him. Kill'd him.

Peter Is there no law to hang her?

Hortensio   Get ye in,
And let her know her misery. I dare not,
For fear impatience seize me, see her more.
Bid her for wifehood,
For honesty, if she have any in her,
Cry if she can; your weeping cannot mend it.
The body will be here presently, so tell her;
And all his friends to curse her.

Peter O Grumio, Grumio!

Grumio	O my worthy master!
Peter	O my most beastly mistress, hang her!
Grumio	Split her.
Peter	Drown her directly.
Grumio	Starve her.
Peter	Stink upon her.

Grumio   Stone her to death. May all she eat be eggs,
Till she run kicking mad for men.

Peter   And
That man that gives her remedy, pray heav'n
He may lose his longings.

Hortensio   Call her out.   *Exit Grumio*

Enter Petronius, Gremio, and Petruchio borne in a coffin

Petronius Set down the body.

Enter Maria in black, and Grumio

You are welcome to the last cast of your fortunes;
There lies your husband, there your loving husband,
There he that was Petruchio, too good for ye;
Your stubborn and unworthy way has kill'd him
Ere he could reach the sea. If ye can weep
Now ye have cause; begin, and after death
Do something yet to th' world, to think ye honest.
So many tears had sav'd him, shed in time
And as they are, so a good mind go with 'em,
Yet they may move compassion.

Maria   Pray ye all hear me,
And judge me as I am, not as you covet,
For that would make me yet more miserable.
'Tis true I have cause to grieve, and mighty cause,
And truly and unfeignedly I weep it.

Hortensio   I see there's some good nature yet left in her.

Maria   But what's the cause? Mistake me not: not this man,
As he is dead, I weep for – heaven defend it,
I never was so childish – but his life,
His poor unmanly wretched foolish life,
Is that my full eyes pity, there's my mourning.

Petronius   Dost thou not shame?

Maria   I do, and even to water,
To think what this man was, to think how simple,
How far below a man, how far from reason,
From common understanding, and all gentry.
He had a happy turn, he died. I'll tell ye,
These are the wants I weep for, not his person.
The memory of this man, had he liv'd
But two years longer, had begot more follies
Than wealthy Autumn flies. But let him rest;
He was a fool, and farewell he.

Petruchio   Unbutton me,
I die indeed else. O Maria,
O my unhappiness, my misery!

Peter   Go to him, whore. I swear, if he perish,
I'll see thee hang'd myself.

Petruchio   Why, why, why, Maria?

Maria   I have done my worst, and have my end: I've tam'd ye,
And now am vow'd your servant. Look not strangely,
Nor fear what I say to you. Dare you kiss me?
Thus I begin my new love.

Petruchio   Once again?

Maria   With all my heart.

Petruchio   Once again, Maria!
O gentlemen, I know not where I am.

Hortensio Get ye to bed then: there you'll quickly know, sir.

Petruchio Never no more your old tricks?

Maria   Never, sir.

Petruchio You shall not need, for as I have a faith,
No cause shall give occasion.

Maria   As I am honest,
And as I am a maid yet all my life
From this hour, since ye make so free profession,
I dedicate in service to your pleasure.

Hortensio Aye, marry, this goes roundly off.

Petruchio   Go, Grumio,
Get all the best meat may be bought for money,
And let the hogshead's blood. I am born again.
Well, little England, when I see a husband
Of any other nation stern or jealous,
I'll wish him but a woman of thy breeding.

Enter Rowland, Livia, Bianca, and Tranio, as from marriage

Petronius What have we here?

Rowland   Another morris, sir,
That you must pipe to.

Tranio   A poor married couple
Desire an offering, sir.

Bianca   Never frown at it,
You cannot mend it now. There's your own hand,
And yours, Gremio, to confirm the bargain.

Petronius My hand?

Gremio   Or mine?

Bianca   You'll find it so.

Petronius   A trick!
I swear, a trick!

Bianca   Yes sir, we trick'd ye.

Livia   Father.

Petronius Hast thou lain with him? Speak!

Livia   Yes truly, sir.

Petronius And hast thou done the deed, boy?

Rowland   I have done, sir,
That that will serve the turn, I think.

Petruchio   A match then.
I'll be the maker up of this. Gremio,
There's now no remedy, you see; be willing,
For be or be not, he must have the wench.

Gremio Since I am overreach'd, let's in to dinner,
And if I can, I'll drink't away.

Tranio   That's well said.

Petronius Well, sirrah, you have play'd a trick. Look to't,
And let me be a grandsire within's twelve-month,
Or by this hand, I'll curtail half your fortunes.

Rowland There shall not want my labour, sir. Your money
Here's one has undertaken.

Tranio   Well, I'll trust her,
And glad I have so good a pawn.

Rowland   I'll watch ye.

Petruchio Let's in, and drink of all hands, and be jovial.
I have my colt again, and now she carries;
And gentlemen, whoever marries next,
Let him be sure he keep him to his text.

EPILOGUE

Maria   *The tamer's tam'd. But so as nor the men*
Can find one just cause to complain of when
They fitly do consider in their lives
They should not reign as tyrants o'er their wives,
Nor can the women from this precedent
Insult or triumph, it being aptly meant
To teach both sexes due equality;
And, as they stand bound, to love mutually
If this effect, arising from a cause
Well laid and grounded, may deserve applause,
We something more than hope our honest ends
Will keep the men, and women too, our friends.

FINIS